Robot Invasion
7 Cool and Easy
Robot Projects

About the Author

Dave Johnson writes about sorts of fun technology from his home in Colorado. He's the Editor of *Handheld Computing's Mobility* magazine and writes a free weekly electronic newsletter on digital photography for *PC World* magazine. In addition, he's the author of two dozen books that include *How to Use Digital Video, How to Do Everything with MP3 and Digital Music,* and *How to Do Everything with Your Palm Handheld* (the latter two with Rick Broida; all McGraw-Hill/Osborne). His short story for early readers, *The Wild Cookie,* has been transformed into an interactive storybook on CD-ROM.

Dave started writing professionally in 1990, before anyone had a chance to talk him out of it. Prior to that, he had a somewhat unfocused career that included flying satellites, driving an ice cream truck, managing weapons at an Air Force base, stocking shelves at Quick Check, teaching rocket science, photographing a rock band, and writing about space penguins. He's still not playing bass in a psychedelic rock band, but at least he's found steady work.

About the Technical Editor

Kevin Mukhar has been developing software for robots for several years. Most recently he has been developing mobile smart agents in Java. When he is not writing, either software or books, he is studying for a Master's in Computer Science and learning how to play the saxophone. Someday, maybe he'll be a tenth as good as John Coltrane. His Web site is currently at **http://home.earthlink.net/~kmukhar/**.

Robot Invasion

7 Cool and Easy Robot Projects

Dave Johnson

McGraw-Hill/Osborne

New York   Chicago   San Francisco   Lisbon   London   Madrid   Mexico City
Milan   New Delhi   San Juan   Seoul   Singapore   Sydney   Toronto

The McGraw·Hill Companies

McGraw-Hill/Osborne
2600 Tenth Street
Berkeley, California 94710
U.S.A.

To arrange bulk purchase discounts for sales promotions, premiums, or fund-raisers, please contact **McGraw-Hill**/Osborne at the above address. For information on translations or book distributors outside the U.S.A., please see the International Contact Information page immediately following the index of this book.

Robot Invasion: 7 Cool and Easy Robot Projects

1234567890 QPD QPD 0198765432

ISBN 0-07-222640-4

Publisher
Brandon A. Nordin

Vice President & Associate Publisher
Scott Rogers

Acquisitions Editor
Margie McAneny

Project Editor
Mark Karmendy

Acquisitions Coordinator
Tana Allen

Technical Editor
Kevin Mukhar

Copy Editor
Susie Elkind

Proofreader
Pat Mannion

Indexer
Jack Lewis

Computer Designer
Carie Abrew

Illustrators
Melinda Lytle, Michael Mueller, Lyssa Wald

Series Design
Carie Abrew, Jean Butterfield

Cover Design
Pattie Lee

This book was composed with Corel VENTURA™ Publisher.

*This book is for my best friend, Paul,
who taught me that when a circuit
has heated to 50,000 degrees, it matters
little whether you're measuring
temperature in Celsius or Rankine.*

Contents at a Glance

Contents

Acknowledgments

Thanks to everyone that made this book a blast to write. Those include:

Kevin, whose programming expertise was instrumental to completing Project 5. Let me put this another way: without Kevin Mukhar, a great, great friend and programmer extraordinaire, there would have been no Project 5.

Paul and **Aaron**, who helped me brainstorm the physics and engineering of several projects.

Margie McAneny, the world's best editor—who thought enough of me to bring this book idea to me in the first place.

My daughter, **Marin**, for locking me out of the house when I was testing Project 4, forcing me to break into the house "Lethal Weapon style" through a side door.

My cat, **Hobbes**, for crying like a misaligned warp core whenever I was on the phone.

… and everyone else on the Osborne team. I have already thanked Kevin Mukhar for his programming help, but he was also excellent as a tech editor (though, for next time, Kevin, remember this: *make two comments per chapter, not two comments per paragraph!*). Tana Allen was wonderful to work with as always. Mark Karmendy was an excellent project editor. And Carie Abrew, Jean Butterfield, Lyssa Wald, Melinda Lytle, and Michael Mueller turned this into the best-looking book I've ever been associated with. Wow, it really looks just awesome.

A World of Robots

As a kid growing up in the 1960s and 1970s, the 21st century seemed very exciting and futuristic to me. After calculating if I'd still be alive in the year 2001 (it turned out that I'd be pretty old—in my 30s—but, I assumed, still able to enjoy the wonders of futuristic technology), I dreamed of living with robot maids, robot cars, robot teachers, and all the other robots that would surely be a part of our lives.

Guess what? Here we are in the 21st century and those robots haven't caught up with us yet.

That's okay, because there are different kinds of robots instead. There really are a lot of robots in the world around us; you just have to know where to look. Robots work in factories, making the everyday stuff we buy in stores and use at home. Robots help manage traffic on railroad tracks and in city streets. Robots help scientists, rescue workers, and police deal with dangerous situations. Robots land on other planets and help us explore outer space. And robots even make appearances on television every day in Gladiator-like battles for our own entertainment. They don't hover in mid-air while flipping our morning pancakes, but they do some pretty amazing things anyway.

What Is a Robot?

With so many different kinds of robots around us, some people wonder what, exactly, defines a robot. Is a robot remote controlled by a human being? Is it

autonomous (which means it can make decisions and control itself)? Does a robot need to be able to move, or can it be bolted to the ground and still be a robot?

These are excellent questions, because robots come in all shapes and sizes, and you can easily find examples of all kinds of robots. The American Heritage Dictionary defines a robot this way:

An externally manlike mechanical device capable of performing human tasks or behaving in a human manner.

That's one way to look at a robot, but it's not a very complete definition. That would mean that in order to be a robot, something would have to look or act like a human. What about robots that look like cars, planes, bugs, and dogs? In the 1970s, the Robot Institute of America said that this was the definition of a robot:

A robot is a reprogrammable, multifunction manipulator designed to move material, parts, tools, or specialized devices through various programmed motions for the performance of a variety of tasks.

That is a definition that covers a lot of different kinds of robots. In fact, it can describe a robotic arm that welds car parts together or searches for minerals at the bottom of the ocean...but it still kinda sounds like our good old maid-bot. The maid robot is programmable, it manipulates things, and it can perform a variety of different tasks. And when you think about it, that's what most people think of when they picture a robot in their heads. But robots don't have to operate without help from humans. Take a look at some of these robots which are controlled more or less continuously by people:

✔ **Mars Pathfinder** In 1996, NASA sent a rover robot to Mars to explore the planet and investigate the Martian environment. Because it had a long, flat solar array on top, the Pathfinder looked like a futuristic skateboard. Pathfinder was a robot, but it was controlled from earth. It didn't make its own decisions about where to go or what rocks to sample. Instead, scientists at NASA told Pathfinder what to do every time it moved or looked at something.

✔ **Battlebots** You've probably seen the TV show called Battlebots. These robots don't make any decisions on their own. A human being with a remote control steers the robot, tells it when to use its weapon, and tries to keep it from getting pushed into the hazards. Is this a robot? Some people would say it isn't—it's just a fancy remote control car.

But many modern robots work this way today, including Andros.

✔ **Andros** The police department in Hartford, Connecticut, uses a robot called Andros to help their bomb squad defuse dangerous explosives without endangering people. The bomb squad operates Andros via remote control. And though it's considered a state of the art robot, Andros does very little on its own—it relies on people to steer it, operate its arms, and handle the explosives.

Robots don't even have to be made of hardware. They can be completely virtual, living as a program inside a computer's memory. People often use programs called *bots* to do special tasks automatically. On the Internet, for instance, bots can be programmed to search for certain information on web pages or to help catalog a vast number of web sites very quickly. Some search engines even base their online "personality" around the software robot that does the searches. Lycos has its Hotbot search engine, for instance.

Some programs use the principles of robotics to automate boring tasks. Imagine, for a moment, that you are a painter living in the 24th century. You get a call from someone who wants to show off all of your paintings—but they need to be smaller and have a blue border around them. You could call your robot assistant and tell it to do the hard work for you. Some computer programs, like Image Robot, from a company called Jasc, do exactly that (check out Figure 1). You can tell the program what kind of changes to make, and then load a hundred or a thousand digital images and let it work—while you go eat lunch or watch television. Mail merge software is another kind of software robot. By feeding a large number of names and addresses into a mail merge program, you can automatically customize a form letter so that it's personally addressed to each person, and the program can print address labels for each letter as well.

Figure 1
It may not look like a robot, but software can certainly behave like a robot, doing repetitive tasks for you.

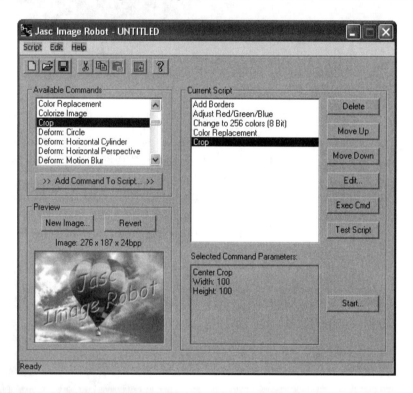

Can Robots Think?

In every science fiction movie from *Star Wars* to *Star Trek* and everything in between, robots are almost always depicted as being smart, thinking, sometimes emotional machines. It's almost as if people take for granted that robots will someday be able to think just like people.

For the moment, robots certainly have no capacity for thought. Like a desktop computer, a mechanical printing press, or a microwave oven, robots are designed to perform a specific series of tasks and they have no understanding of what they are actually doing.

Robots can start to deceive us, though, when they begin to look like living things. Movie makers often make robots look bad or "evil" by putting them in insect form—most folks just don't like bugs, and that's all it takes to make us think the robots are bad. Make the bug out of metal and it's even creepier. Likewise, robot pets like the Sony Aibo are cute enough to fool us into petting and cooing over them. We may realize with the intellectual part of our brain that a robot dog isn't really a dog, but we'll pet it anyway. If you throw in the fact that a programmer designed the robot to act like a dog with realistic animal behavior, we can easily get distressed when the robot acts like it is sad or hurt or depressed.

If a robot is built in human form, things get even more confusing. If the robot is programmed to act like it has emotions, we might be inclined to believe—or at least want to believe—that the robot has real human feelings. In reality, the robot may not feel anything at all. It's just a very sophisticated can opener that has been programmed to act human. Consider the movie *AI*. The little robot boy in the film certainly acted human. He seemed to have emotions, and people in the movie confused him for a real boy. But does that make him really have emotions? It's hard to tell. In an episode of *Star Trek: The Next Generation*, a lawyer from Starfleet tried to take away the rights of the robot crewmember named Data by arguing that he was treated as human only because he acted human. He then turned off Data by flipping a switch. Can we treat robots as equals if we have the ability to just turn them off?

How will we know if a robot is really thinking and not just acting out its program? That's a question that philosophers, scientists, and technology experts are trying to answer right now. We may need to know the answer to that question within our lifetime, since some experts believe computers may possibly begin to think for themselves around the year 2050, when computer processors reach the same level of complexity as the human brain.

So, in the year 2055, when your robot maid tells you it is sad that it never gets a day off, you might have to believe it's telling you the truth. When that happens, will you agree with the politicians who want to give computers equal rights—or with the politicians who don't?

Robots Around Us

An appliance company called Sunbeam is pioneering household robots that will do everything but wash the dog. Various gadgets automatically brew coffee before you get out of bed, track your weight every time you use a bathroom scale, and reset all the clocks in the house after a power failure.

Robomower is an autonomous mower that navigates its way around your lawn and cuts grass all by itself. It has an electric motor and senses the edge of your lawn by looking for low-voltage "guide wires" that are buried under the ground.

Aibo is a robot pet from Sony that mimics many of the ordinary behaviors of a dog or cat. Aibo is programmed to experience "moods," explore the house, play with toys, and respond to the sound of your voice.

You can buy a robot called Cye from Probotics. Cye is a robot with wheels, an Internet connection, and a digital camera. You can drive it around your house and see what's happening from any computer in the world, as long as it has a modem.

So Where Did Robots Start?

Robots have been around a lot longer than you might realize. Leonardo da Vinci envisioned his own robot, and some people believe he actually built it as long ago as 1495. His design was a robotic knight that used a complicated array of gears and pulleys to perform for spectators by sitting up, waving its arms, and moving its head—not unlike the robot-like characters you'll find in many amusement parks. They're called "animatronic," and they're lifelike figures programmed to perform the same actions over and over again.

It wasn't until the 1950s that people started building robots for practical applications—like the automated machines in factories that we take for granted today. But the word robot itself has been around since the very start of the 20th century. Czech playwright Karel Capek wrote a play in 1921 called R. U. R. It stood for Rossum's Universal Robots, and the play was about the problems that occurred when an army of mechanical workers replaced human factory workers. Here's a brief timeline of some of the most interesting developments in the field of robotics:

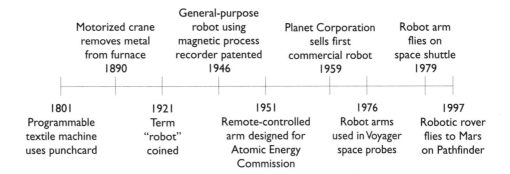

Motorized crane removes metal from furnace
1890

General-purpose robot using magnetic process recorder patented
1946

Planet Corporation sells first commercial robot
1959

Robot arm flies on space shuttle
1979

1801
Programmable textile machine uses punchcard

1921
Term "robot" coined

1951
Remote-controlled arm designed for Atomic Energy Commission

1976
Robot arms used in Voyager space probes

1997
Robotic rover flies to Mars on Pathfinder

What's Inside a Robot?

Robots tend to vary quite a bit. As you've already seen, robots can be bolted to a tabletop or drive around under their own power. They might be programmed to look for minerals on a strange planet or to stack objects in a sorting machine. But in general, we can say that all mechanical robots are made with four major parts:

✔ Base
✔ Processor
✔ Actuators
✔ Sensors

Asimov's Three Laws of Robotics

Famous science fiction writer Isaac Asimov was one of the first people to put a friendly, helpful face on robots. In a 1942 story called Runaround, Asimov invented three laws which governed the behavior of all of the robots in his story. The three laws are

✔ A robot may not injure a human being, or, through inaction, allow a human being to come to harm.

✔ A robot must obey orders given it by human beings, except where such orders would conflict with the First Law.

✔ A robot must protect its own existence as long as such protection does not conflict with the First or Second Law.

Isaac Asimov would later find these three laws so useful that he based many of his books on the premise that robots of the future were built and programmed to obey these three laws. Asimov's Laws have found their way into many books written by other authors, and even into movies and television shows.

Actually creating a robot to follow the three laws is very, very difficult. The robot would have to be able to predict the outcome of its actions, something that's well beyond today's technology. Someday, though, robots may be programmed to try to anticipate the consequences of their actions and avoid doing things that would hurt human beings.

The Base

A robot's base is its body. It can be stationary—which means it is mounted in one place and cannot move around—or it can have a mobile body. Mobile robots come in a vast number of forms. Commonly, robots have wheels to roll around like cars—but there are also many robots with other, more exotic ways of moving around.

Believe it or not, some robots swim. At the engineering school MIT, for instance, students are building a "Robot Pike," which is designed to swim around just like a fish. Then there are robot snakes, which have a long body made of lots of little segments that help the bot slither around in situations—like mushy sand or even outer space—where traditional wheels wouldn't work very well.

One of the most popular but difficult systems for getting robots to move is with legs. Robots come with all manner and arrangements of legs, from six- and eight-legged insect-like bodies (such as in Figure 2) to two-legged, human-like forms. Hexplorer 2000 is a six-legged walker that was designed at the University of Waterloo in Canada. Why would someone make a robot with six legs? Mainly to create an efficient walking robot—making a robot walk reliably is tricky, but using multiple legs is easier than walking upright on just two. There are also practical applications. A six-legged robot like Hexplorer can walk over uneven, rugged terrain much more easily than a robot on wheels or on two legs.

Figure 2
Multilegged robots look creepy, but they're much more stable than robots with two legs (they're harder to knock over), and they can go places that wheeled robots have trouble navigating.

Two-legged robots that walk more or less like people are fiendishly difficult to design. You'd be surprised at the amount of effort it takes our human brain to allow us to walk around on uneven ground, climb stairs, and do other seemingly-simple tasks. One of the earliest two-legged robots is a guy named Timmy that runs in Harvard's robot lab. Timmy can't leave the lab, because he can only walk in circles around a big post. More recently, other two-legged robots have been more mobile. Lurch is a seven-foot-tall walking robot from the University of Alabama, and Pinocchio is a much smaller walking robot whose body is made from a plastic bucket and whose feet are just plain old soup bowls. Despite the silly body, the robot is smart enough to walk around unassisted. Perhaps the most impressive two-legged robot around is Asimo, designed by Honda (see Figure 3). Asimo is a life-sized humanoid robot that looks very much like someone in a space suit. Asimo is perhaps the most sophisticated two-legged robot ever made, able to walk unassisted and even negotiate stairs—something no other two-legged robot has ever done.

Figure 3
Asimo is one of the most advanced two-legged robots in the world. It can walk naturally and climb stairs without help from humans.

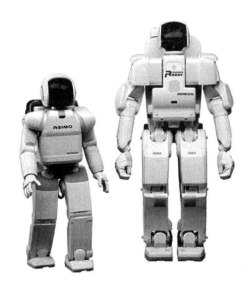

The Processor

If a robot is to be smart enough to get around or make decisions on its own, it needs a processor. A processor is a computer that acts as the robot's brain.

Depending upon the size of the robot, the processor can be large or small, fast or slow. A very small robot may not have room for a big, fast computer processor, so it might have to rely on a fairly simple computer chip that can't make the kinds of decisions the robot would need to navigate complex environments or perform difficult tasks. Imagine a robot that is trying to find its way around a strange place, for instance. The processor would need to be able to react quickly enough to keep the robot out of danger, such as from falling off a cliff or getting flipped upside down.

Robots with a stationary base don't have to worry about this kind of problem, because the processor can be very, very large—and can be connected via a cable from another room, if necessary. Choosing a computer that's good enough to operate mobile robots that have to balance issues like battery power

and overall size, but is not so big or power-hungry that the robot can't travel far, is always a problem.

Actuators and Sensors

In the "robot" that is the human body, your eyes, ears, and nose are sensors, while your muscles are actuators that let you respond to the things you see, hear, and smell around you.

Of course, not all robots have sensors. A very simple assembly-line robot that never has to "find" the parts it is working on may not need to sense the world around it. But more advanced robots, and certainly most robots of our future, have a need for sensors to tell them where to walk, how to avoid bumping into things and people, and what to do next.

Robots can make use of sensors that mimic ordinary human senses. Sensors can be sensitive to light, touch, heat, sound, smell, and even taste (check out Figure 4). But there's no reason to stop there, and many robots are attuned to radar and sonar, acceleration and speed, electricity, and more. If the robot has a satellite navigation sensor (called a GPS receiver), it can even determine its location, accurate to within a few feet, anywhere on the planet.

Figure 4
Even "toy" robots like Lego MindStorms and the Sony Aibo are getting sophisticated enough to come with sensors that can help the robots move around on their own.

Whether a robot has sensors or not, almost all robots need some kind of actuators, since actuators are what make a robot move. Actuators move arms and legs, make wheels turn, and make claws or hands open and close. Actuators can be motors or servos, or simple "muscle wires." Muscle wires are a fascinating way to make robots move. Actually called Nitinol, muscle wires contract when heated and expand when cooled. If you run an electrical current through a strand of

Nitinol to change its temperature, you can use it like a human muscle to move a robot leg. Many robots have been made with Nitinol as an actuator, and you can build your own version of a walking robot by buying some Nitinol or a walking-robot kit. One of the most popular robot kits with muscle wire is called Stiquito.

Putting It All Together

A robot's processor can't figure out where it's going all by itself. Someone needs to program the robot with basic instructions. The processor can then interpret the instructions to accomplish whatever task it was intended to do. The processor can send signals to the actuator, for instance, to navigate a route between two points, or to pick up an object, perform a task with it, and put it down in the right location when it's done.

The more complicated the task, the more likely the robot will need sensors to interpret its surroundings. If a robot is supposed to navigate a route, for instance, it might be able to do that just fine without sensors, as long as the route is always exactly the same and there are never any obstacles in the way. If the robot needs to pause for through-traffic or find an object that isn't always in exactly the same place, that's where visual and touch sensors come in handy.

Try it yourself. Imagine you are a robot programmer and you want a robot to find its way from one end of your house to the other. Use a volunteer—like dad or a friend—to play the part of the robot. Blindfold your "robot" and give directions to reach the destination only in words that can be understood by someone who can't see or feel anything. Want to add a visual sensor to your robot? Take the blindfold off, and then you can give your "robot" much more powerful commands, like "Walk forward until you see the wall." Without a sensor, you'll have to make your robot walk just a few steps at a time so no one gets hurt!

Even with sensors, actuators, and a processor, it's not easy to make a robot perform tasks that most people take for granted. Programming a robot to cook you breakfast, for instance, includes breaking an egg. Your robot would need extremely sensitive touch sensors and gentle actuators in order to pick the egg up without breaking it. The vision sensors would need to be good enough to manipulate utensils, and you'd also need to give the robot very advanced sensors to know when the eggs were done cooking. As if all that weren't enough, the robot wouldn't be able to follow a rigid program like an assembly-line robot in a factory. Instead, the robot would need to have a sophisticated "artificial intelligence" program that would allow it to deduce things about its task from the environment and adapt to problems that may crop up during the day—like how to get eggshells out of the frying pan, how to identify a spoiled egg, and what to do if the egg accidentally falls on the floor. As you can see, making a robot can be a very complicated task.

Catching Robots with a Neural Net

Traditional programming usually means telling a robot how to deal with every situation it might encounter in painstaking detail. But that's not a very good way of making robots: If you expect a housecleaning robot to work around your house or a firefighter robot to find its way around town on its own, robots need to be able to deduce things about their environment based on a general set of rules, not millions and millions of specific instructions that take a long time to program.

That's where neural networks come in. Neural networks are computer programs that try to mimic the way the human brain works by behaving like the millions of neurons in our heads. While scientists haven't mastered the art of creating computerized neural networks, they seem to show a lot of promise. Neural networks are great for robots because they adapt—they constantly learn from the robot's experiences and get better with time. Neural networks also are good at drawing conclusions about specific situations based on a more general set of guidelines. A robot with a neural network can read text from any newspaper because it can learn to recognize the letter "A" no matter how it is drawn or printed, for instance. Or it might be able to understand that all the vehicles on the street are cars, while a traditional robot might only be able to recognize those cars that look exactly like the ones it was programmed to recognize. So the robots that wash your car and walk your dog in a few years will probably think a lot like you do—thanks to neural networks.

PROJECT 1

Robot Racers

What You'll Need

Lego MindStorms Robotic Invention System 2.0. You can build the robot with an older set, but some of the steps will be slightly different, and you'll have to improvise!

- ✔ Foam board, at least 32×40 inches
- ✔ Lego blocks
- ✔ Some quarters
- ✔ Electrical tape (½-inch wide)
- ✔ Black construction paper
- ✔ Pencil
- ✔ Hobby knife
- ✔ Scissors
- ✔ Drawing compass
- ✔ Glue

Time Required

About 8 hours

Difficulty

Not hard. You can probably do most of this on your own, but you might want a parent around to help cut the foam board accurately.

Project

Build a four-wheeled robot using the Lego MindStorms. You will program it to perform sort of a robotic obstacle course—it will drive around to find a small block, and then push it along a path. The robot will dump it into a goal, turn around, and get another block to repeat the course. You can use this robot to compete against another robot to see who can run the course the fastest. If you only have one robot, you and a friend can take turns modifying the robot to see who can make the best design.

Introduction

Welcome to our first project together. In Project 1, we're going to assemble a robot using a Lego MindStorms kit. It's easy to build, but will do a few very interesting things—it follows a path, moves blocks around, and, most importantly, can be used in a race against another person. As you'll see, you can race someone that has built a similar robot, or you can time your robot as it runs the course and then let your opponent change the bot and race again.

What Are MindStorms?

Lego sells a special robots version of its building blocks called Lego MindStorms. The basic MindStorms set includes all the stuff you need to make your own robots, either from plans or from scratch. It includes about 700 pieces, including hardware like motors, touch and light sensors, and all the gears and connecting pieces you need for some very cool designs. After you build the robot, you can program it with a very easy-to-use programming language on the PC. You simply drag command "blocks" around on the PC screen to tell the robot to move, stop, turn, pick things up, make decisions, and more. If you have just gotten Lego MindStorms, follow the computer lessons to learn how it all works, and build at least one or two robots from the Lego plans—then come back here and try your hand at the robot racers.

The Robot

Our robot will start from its very own parking spot and move into the Starting Circle, where it will find its first Cargo Box. You'll be in charge of adding the Cargo Boxes to the race area, but if you really wanted to, it wouldn't be too hard to make a separate "box tender" robot that did this automatically for us throughout the race!

The goal is for the robot to grab the Cargo Box and begin pushing it around. It needs to find the curvy race path all by itself and follow the path to the end of the line, where a Goal Hole has been cut in the race area. The robot should drop its cargo into the hole, turn around, and follow the path back to the starting circle, where it'll find the next Cargo Box. Of course, you'll have to put it there after the robot leaves with the first Cargo Box. Check out Figure 1-1 for a look at the course.

Figure 1-1
You'll make a race course out of a large foam board and see who can push blocks to the end of the course the fastest.

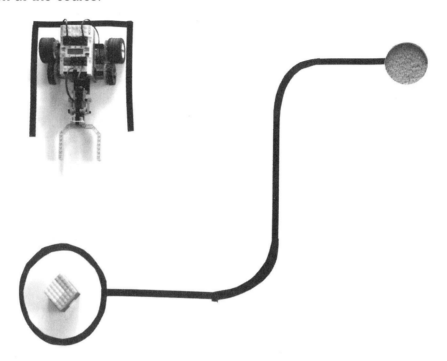

After taking possession of a Cargo Box, the robot needs to turn around, get back on the path, and drop it through the hole. It can do this as many times as you want. If you're racing your robot, you probably want to set up special rules, like, "Which robot can push three Cargo Boxes through the Goal Hole the fastest?" I'll get you started with a robot that can perform well, but if you want to win, it's up to you to tweak the robot for better performance.

Because of the way this robot moves around on the race course, I've named him **Sweeper**. So don't be confused when I talk about Sweeper—I mean the guy we're about to build.

The Plan

We'll have to build Sweeper and program it using the MindStorms programming language. We'll also have to build a few cargo boxes and make the racetrack as well. If you have a second Lego MindStorms kit (or have a friend who does), you can make two Sweepers and compete side-by-side. If you only have access to one kit, that's okay—you can take turns modifying and competing with your robot.

Building the Robot

Let's start with the robot itself. Sweeper is based on the standard Lego MindStorms Roverbot, which is built by following the instructions for the Driving Base (look at Figure 1-1 for a reminder of what the Driving Base looks like) in the Lego Constructopedia (which, of course, is the book that comes with your Lego MindStorms). Go ahead and make the Roverbot Driving Base and then we'll add to it to make Sweeper. I'll wait right here until you're done.

Figure 1-2
Remember the Driving Base? You'll need to build it to make Sweeper.

Make the Sensor Pod

Back so soon? Great. With the Roverbot Driving Base complete, we need to add the special equipment that turns this robot into Sweeper. The Roverbot will need two things in order to navigate our racing course: a light sensor for finding and following the racetrack, and a "Sweeping Fork" for pushing the Cargo Box through the track. We'll combine both of these sensors into a single assembly, which we'll call the Sensor Pod, and attach it to the front of the robot. The finished Sensor Pod will look like the one in Figure 1-3.

Figure 1-3
Our Sensor Pod includes both a light sensor (for staying on track) and a touch sensor (so we know when we're pushing the Cargo Box).

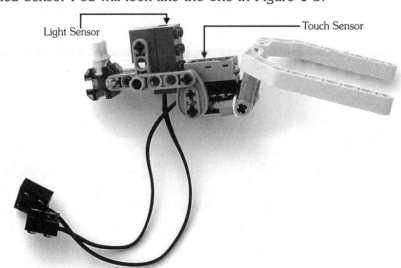

Light Sensor

Touch Sensor

Here's how to build the Sensor Pod:

1. Push a 4X rod through a pair of 2×1 blocks.

2. Add a bracket and the small connectors to one side of the assembly, as you can see here.

3. Add the blue connector that will eventually attach the Sensor Pod to the Roverbot body.

4. Attach the two connectors to the bracket, then push the bracket onto the other side of the assembly. Finally, push a 6X rod through the elbow hole in the two brackets.

5. Take the light sensor and attach it to the pair of 2×1 blocks, with the connection cable running out of the assembly as you can see here.

That's the light sensor—now it's time to add the Sweeping Fork to the front. Set the light sensor aside for a minute; we'll come back to it before you know it.

6. Assemble the parts in the picture shown here on a 4X rod. Hold the assembly together with a small rubber band.

7. Now add two 3X rods to the bottom. Push the pair of rounded blocks onto the 3X rods. You've made the Sweeping Fork's pivot joint assembly. When something touches the Sweeping Fork, it'll push this assembly into the touch sensor.

8. Add a 5X rod, a pair of ovals, and two spacers to the end of the pivot joint assembly.

9. Go get the light sensor assembly and add a bracket to the end of the 6X rod, as shown.

IO. Press a connection wire block onto the touch sensor and set it aside for a moment.

11. Take another 6X rod and carefully slide it slightly through the bottom hole of the oval on the pivot joint assembly. Once it's through the oval, take the touch sensor and position it so its hole lines up with the rod. Continue to push the rod through the oval so it goes through the touch sensor, too. When the rod gets to the oval on the other side of the pivot joint, stop.

12. Now it's time to combine the separate touch sensor and the light sensor assemblies into one Sensor Pod. Orient the 6X rod you've been pushing through the touch sensor so it lines up with the bracket you added to the light sensor assembly in step 9. Push it through. Add another bracket to the other side of the Sensor Pod so it connects the two big rods.

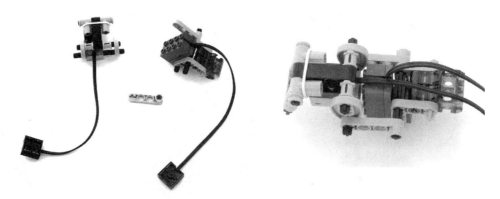

13 Finally, take two bumper arms and attach them to the pivot joint assembly so that they point straight out in front. Instead of being bumpers, they'll tend to catch small objects (like our Cargo Boxes) as the robot drives forward.

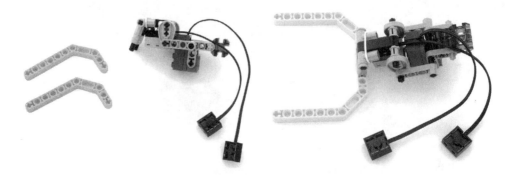

14. Attach the Sensor Pod to the front of the robot using a dual-connector. Plug the touch sensor into sensor port 1 and connect the light sensor into sensor port 2.

Your robot is ready for programming! Before we get to programming, though, we have a few more things to build.

Making Some Cargo Boxes

You're not supposed to "push around" people that are smaller than you, but it's perfectly okay for Sweeper to push some cargo boxes around. After all, the number of boxes it can push into the hole in a certain amount of time is what will determine our race winner.

You can make your cargo boxes any way you like—and out of any material you like. In fact, since your robot will work a little differently than mine and might be racing on a slightly different surface, you may need to modify your design. I suggest that you make your blocks the same way I made mine, though, and change the design later if you need or want to. If you do change the design, be sure that your Cargo Boxes fit easily into the Sweeping Fork, or you'll have a hard time racing.

The cargo box is pretty simple to build. It is a square that's six pegs per side and four blocks high (check out Figure 1-4). The block has a hollow center that's just the right size to hold four quarters. We'll add the quarters to make the Cargo Box the proper weight for our robot to use.

Figure 1-4
We'll be programming Sweeper to push Cargo Boxes like these into the Goal Hole.

Assemble the Cargo Boxes

1. Take one 6×2 and three 4×2 Legos and lay them out like this. This is the base level of our cargo box.

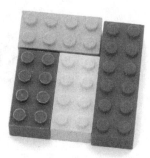

2. Add the second layer. You'll need three 4×2 blocks and one 6×2. Arrange them like this.

3. The third layer is hollow to make room for the quarters. Get two 4×1 blocks and two 6×1 blocks and attach them like this.

4. Take four quarters and place them inside the box. If you want the Cargo Box to weigh the same as mine, you really need four quarters—ten dimes or a silver dollar won't work, even though they all add up to a dollar.

5. Finally, cap the box with a lid that's made from three 6×2 blocks or, if you're short on those bigger blocks, use one 6×2 and three 4×2 Legos.

That's all there is to it. You may want to make at least two of these boxes so it's easier to load the start circle at race time.

Making the Race Course

Now that the robot is complete, it's time to give it somewhere to race. We'll want to make this next, since we need somewhere to test the robot's programming. As you can see from the racetrack in Figure 1-5, the course has four important parts:

Figure 1-5
The course will challenge your Sweeper to stay on track while pushing a payload around, and then know when to turn around and get more.

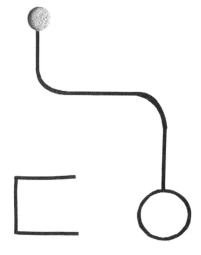

✔ Parking garage

✔ Starting circle

✔ Route

✔ Goal Hole

You'll want to sketch the track on a piece of paper before you start making marks on your expensive foam board (boards cost about $10 each). Take a piece of paper and draw the Starting Circle and Goal Hole, then connect them with a curvy line. You'll want to place both of those locations far enough away from the edge of the paper that your robot will have room to maneuver. It may need to drive forward past the circle, turn, spin, or do other fancy driving to compete in the race. If you put the circle and hole too close to the edge, your poor robot may spend a lot of time falling off the side.

Once you have a fair idea of what you want the course to look like, get the biggest piece of foam board you can get your hands on. Many hobby stores sell big, stiff boards that measure about 32×40 inches. You'll want to get one of those—or even bigger, if you can find it.

Make the Starting Circle

Let's begin by making the Starting Circle.

I. Take a drawing compass and trace a circle on black construction paper that has a radius of about 3 inches.

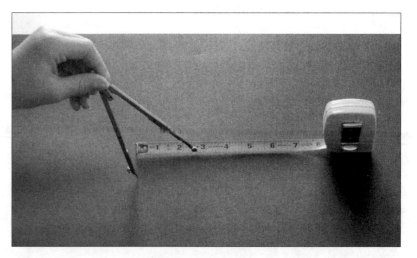

2. Next, trace a second outline that's a little bigger (a radius of about 3 ½ inches), so you've made a "hoop" that's about half an inch thick.

3. Using a pair of scissors, carefully cut along both the inner and outer circles until you have something like this:

4. Take your Starting Circle and lay it on the foam board in its proper place. For starters, you probably want to make sure that the circle doesn't get within about 4 inches of any nearby edge of the board.

5. Finally, use some glue to tack it down to the board.

Cut the Goal Hole

Next, we'll cut the Goal Hole in the foam board, so we'll have made both ends of the route. Take your drawing compass and form the Goal Hole at the opposite corner of the foam board. When you place the Goal Hole, try to make it about 3 ½ inches in diameter and at least 5 inches from any nearby edge of the board.

Next, take a hobby knife and slowly, carefully carve out the hole from the foam. You'll want this to be as smooth and circular as you can make it, so take your time when you cut along the circle you drew with the compass. When you're done, you should be able to push out the middle and end up with a hole. Pay attention to what's under the board while you cut so you don't damage anything valuable!

Tip: *Make sure that the Cargo Box fits easily through the Goal Hole. If it doesn't, make the hole bigger.*

Draw the Route

Now for the moment you've been waiting for! Using a pencil, draw a curvy route that connects the starting and ending point. Once you have a good idea of where the route is going, you're going to take ½-inch-wide black electrical tape and lay it down on the foam board to create a dark line the robot can follow. Don't do it yet, though—I have a few tricks you need to know about.

Electrical tape is good for this kind of project because you can readjust it as you go—if you make a mistake, you can pull the tape up and reapply it to the foam board without tearing up the surface of the board.

You'll probably find that while electrical tape is great for the straight parts of the route, you don't want to make big, sharp curves by laying down tape—the tape will bunch up and get in the robot's way when it tries to drive over the course. For the curves, it's a lot easier to use black construction paper (the same stuff you used to make the Starting Circle). Now that you know what we have planned, it's time to actually do it.

1. Using a ruler or even just gauging the distance by eye, peel off a length of electrical tape that's long enough to cover the first straight stretch of the race route and cut it. Press the tape down on the board, starting at the Starting Circle and ending right about where the first curve starts.

2. Cut another length of tape to pick up after the first curve, where the track gets straight again, and lay it down so it ends right at the start of the second curve. Finally, lay tape down on the third straight line, too. If your racetrack looks like the one in this book, you should have put tape down on all of the straight parts. If you got creative and made a different sort of path, though, go ahead and wrap up any additional straight segments.

3. Now, take a piece of black construction paper and place it on the foam board, where the first curve takes place. Using a pencil, mark the edge of the paper where the two straight segments touch the paper.

4. Draw a smooth curve on the paper to join the two straight segments. If you prefer, you can use a drawing compass to make a perfectly smooth curve instead.

5. Grab the scissors and cut the curve out of the paper. Lay it on the foam board to make sure it joins the two straight parts. If it doesn't, trim the paper until it looks just about right.

6. Finally, glue the construction paper curve to the foam board with a few drops of glue. Let it dry.

7. Add any other curves to the board in the same way.

Add the Parking Garage

The last piece of our race course is the parking garage. You can see that my version is just three pieces of electrical tape in a U pattern—with an open space where Sweeper drives out from. If you prefer, you can change your garage so that there's a definite "starting line" for more official races.

Programming the Robot Racer

Now that Sweeper and all of its accessories are ready, we can try our hand at programming the robot. If you've already made some robots with the Lego MindStorms system, you'll probably have a pretty easy time with this. Even if you're brand new to the idea of writing a computer program, I think you'll see that it's not terribly difficult. Just imagine that your robot is something that can only find its way around by doing exactly what you tell it.

Envision the Program

Instead of rushing into the Robot Invention System software, it helps to start by outlining what we expect Sweeper to do. Go ahead and put the robot in its parking spot and put a Cargo Box in the Starting Circle. Let's pretend we're racing so we can figure out everything that the robot has to do.

1. Start moving out of the parking garage.

2. Move in a straight line until you encounter the Cargo Box in the Starting Circle. You'll know you have found the Cargo Box—you guessed it—when you feel a press on the touch sensor.

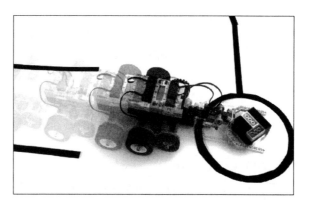

3. Once you have a box in your Sweeping Fork, you can start looking for the race route. You'll probably have the best luck if you make a left turn.

4. Find and follow the route.

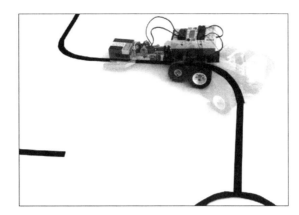

5. How do you know when you've reached the end of the route? With luck, you'll push the Cargo Box into the Goal Hole. When that happens—again, you guessed it—there won't be anything touching the touch sensor.

6. Turn around and find the route back to the Starting Circle.

7. When you reach the Starting Circle, you'll need to turn completely around so you can follow the route back to the Goal Hole.

And that's pretty much it. You can probably already see that once we get to step 4, the race program is really just a big loop. We need to get the robot reliably working from step 4 to step 7, and then after that, we can tell the program to repeat those steps over and over. If you were writing this program on your own, it might help to get out a sheet of paper and write all of the tasks we talked about (find the box, turn, follow the route), each in its own little box, so you don't get confused. In this case, though, I'm here to help you put it all together.

Start the Robotics Invention System software and enter the programming part of the program. When the program asks what kind of robot you want to program, choose to work with a Roverbot.

Find the Cargo Box

The very beginning of the program is quite simple. We simply want to move forward until we touch the Cargo Box, right? So drag the Forward box from the Big Blocks into your program. This command tells the robot to go forward—but we only want it to move forward until it touches something (and hopefully that something is a Cargo Box). So we need a Repeat command, too. Drag Repeat... Until into the program and then put the Forward box inside it.

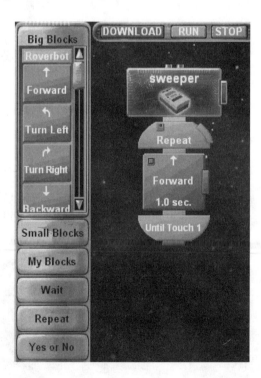

Make sure that the Repeat command is set to look for a "touch" on sensor port 1. Also, change the forward distance to a very small number. We want to stop going forward as soon as we find the Cargo Box, so change the Forward time to .1 seconds.

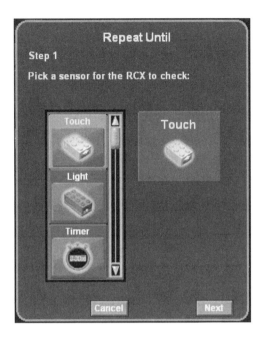

As soon as the robot thinks it has touched the box, we want it to make a 90-degree turn to the left—that should put it close to the track. Drag a Turn Left box onto the program and put it under (not inside) the Repeat... Until box. Since we can't tell Sweeper to turn a certain number of degrees, we have to program it to turn for a certain amount of time. My Sweeper took about 2 seconds to turn on my foam board, but you'll have to experiment to find the right number for your own Sweeper.

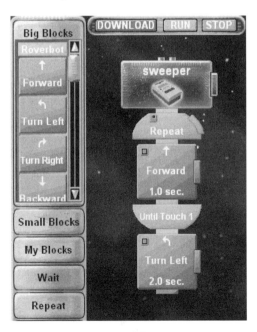

You can test your program now if you want to make sure it works more or less correctly.

Test Your Program

Any time that you add a new command or set of commands to your program, you may want to test it to make sure nothing has gone horribly wrong. If you wait too long to test a program, it becomes hard to know which commands are responsible for the fact that your robot juggles bananas instead of moving in a straight line. If you make a change and test it right away, you have a better chance of fixing small problems before they become really big, annoying problems.

To test your program, turn the robot on and position it near the MindStorms transmitter tower. Click the Download button at the top of the screen, and after the robot beeps, you can put the robot on the race track and click Run to see how well it does. In my robotics lab, I leave the transmitter tower close enough to the racetrack so that I don't have to keep moving the robot back and forth every time I want to test a new part of the program.

Drop Off the Cargo

The next phase of the program is just a little tricky. Look back to our original notes—what do we want Sweeper to do now? If you recall, we want to follow the route until we drop off the Cargo Box into the hole. Let's just work on that piece of the puzzle first, and worry about what to do after the Cargo Box is gone later.

You probably already know how to make a robot follow a black line—it's one of the early training challenges you played with when you first got your MindStorms kit. The subroutine (the name we use for a group of commands in a program), which forces the robot to always move along the edge of the black line, looks like this:

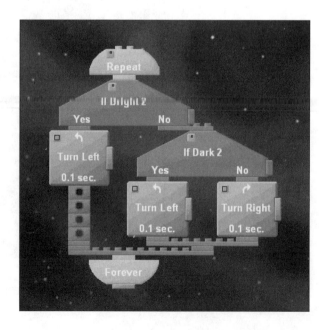

But we can't use that subroutine just the way it is, since it would try to find the black line forever. We want our robot to stay on the line only until it's no longer pushing the Cargo Box. There's an easy fix: Remove the Repeat... Forever command and instead put the rest of the subroutine inside a command that checks to see if the touch sensor is still pressed.

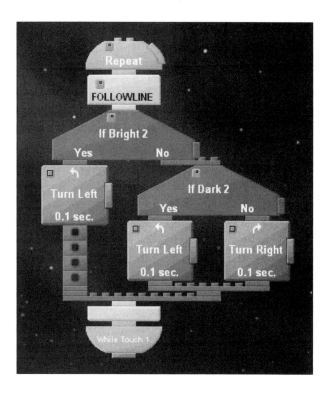

Tip: *To make the program look more organized, I've taken the follow-the-black-line subroutine and made it a specially-named My Block called FollowLine.*

If you try this part of the program right now, though, you'll discover a problem. As soon as Sweeper starts to push the Cargo Box around, they don't always stay in direct contact. And that means the very first time the program checks to see if the touch sensor is pressed, the Cargo Box won't be there—it'll be almost, but not quite touching the touch sensor—so Sweeper will think it has already dropped the box off down into the hole. Game over.

Don't worry. There's an easy way to fix this problem. We just need to calm Sweeper down a bit, and tell it to be patient. Here's the message we want to give to Sweeper:

Check to see if you still have a grip on the Cargo Box. If it seems like there's nothing there, keep driving for a bit and check again. But if you check a few times and there's never anything at the touch sensor, then you can assume that the Cargo Box has gone down the hole.

So how do you do that? With a counter, of course!

Here's what the new, improved subroutine looks like. As we move along the track, we perform the FollowLine subroutine and add one to the counter if the touch sensor isn't being pressed. If it is touched, we still follow the line with FollowLine, but also set the counter back to zero. When the counter reaches a number high enough that it probably means the Cargo Box is really gone, then we end that subroutine and move on.

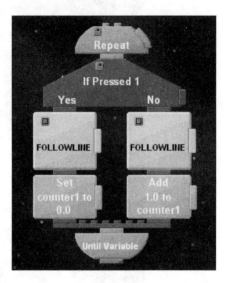

What number is high enough? This is another one of those things that will take some experimentation. As you can see here, I set Sweeper's upper limit to 22. If the counter reaches 22 without sensing a Cargo Box on the touch sensor, Sweeper assumes it has reached the Goal Hole. You might be able to set your number lower—and if you can, your robot will be faster than mine. Do you see how you can tweak your robot to run the course faster?

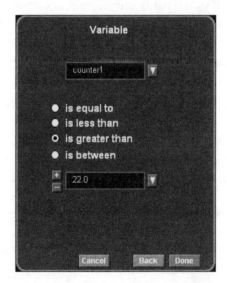

34

Time to Turn Around

This part is easy. If the Cargo Box is gone, just turn around and start looking for the black line again. In my program, I've told Sweeper to back up for a few seconds, then make a right turn. After that, it's probably close enough to the black line that the FollowLine subroutine can latch onto the route and take it back to the Starting Circle.

How does Sweeper know when it has reached the Starting Circle? That's simple—if you weren't asleep, watching TV, or mesmerized by the robot, you probably remembered to put another Cargo Box in the circle. If there's one there, Sweeper should find it. The trick, of course, is to put the FollowLine subroutine into a Repeat... Until box, and program it to repeat until it touches something. So, this part of the program should look something like this.

After Sweeper reaches Repeat... Until and touches the Cargo Box, it's time to turn around and make your way back to the Goal Hole. Just add a Spin box and tell Sweeper to turn long enough so that it turns all the way around and is facing the black line again. This batch of commands is what Sweeper will do from the moment it drops the Cargo Box.

From here, it's exactly the same as when Sweeper made that first left turn back when it found the first Cargo Box. So add a Repeat... For box and put everything that happens after the left turn inside it. Set the Repeat to any number you like... 1, 5, or even 10.

If you test Sweeper now, you might run into a glitch. When the robot spins in the Start Circle, it may turn so fast that it "whips" the Cargo Box out of the arena and bumps your cat on the nose. Not only will your cat not appreciate it, but Sweeper will again be confused and think it has already reached the Goal Hole.

35

To avoid that problem, slow down. Just before you start your spin, go to the Small Blocks and lower the robot's power level to a low number like 1, 2, or 3. Since the robot spins much more slowly, it can hold onto the Cargo Box much more easily. After the spin, don't forget to restore the power to full—or someone else's robot will almost certainly beat you. Don't forget: Since the robot is moving more slowly, you'll have to make the spin time longer for it to go all the way around. That'll take some experimenting!

So what does the entire program look like, from top to bottom? Figure 1-6 shows you. Check it out to make sure you didn't miss an important step! After you've finished the program, be sure to download it to your robot.

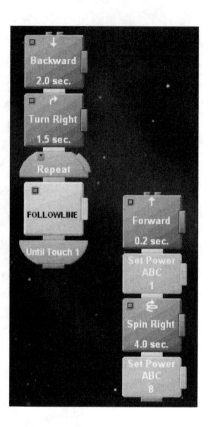

Running the Race

That's it! To test the entire program or run the race, you'll need to set the Goal Hole over the edge of a table so the Cargo Boxes can fall through, or you can prop the goal-end of the foam board up with wooden blocks or Legos. Don't worry—Sweeper has no trouble going up an incline. If you let the boxes fall through from a table-top, put something soft underneath to catch them, or they'll shatter into lots of little Lego blocks when they hit the hard floor.

The Cargo Boxes work best when you put them upside-down on the board—with the pegs facing down (see Figure 1-7). You can try them the other way, but you'll probably find that they tend to get snagged on the tape and construction paper.

You'll want to appoint one person to keep time with a stopwatch. Take Sweeper and put it in its parking spot. When you press the Run button, start the timer and time how many Cargo Boxes can be pushed into the Goal Hole in a certain amount of time, like five minutes. Or, see how long it takes to put three Cargo Boxes in the hole.

Figure I-6
The complete
Sweeper program

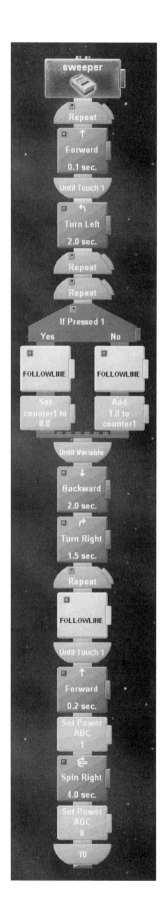

37

Figure I-7
Turn your Cargo
Boxes upside down
for best results.

Improving Your Robot Racer

You already have a competitive robot, but there are things you can do to improve your score. Think about how you can make Sweeper better. Here are some areas of the program you might want to experiment with:

✔ Change the time increment in your movement commands. If you currently go forward .1 seconds at a time, could you get a better score by going forward .01 or .2 seconds at a time? Which is better?

✔ Fine-tune your turn. Are you turning too far, or not far enough? That might make your robot waste time looking for the route. You might be able to help your robot find the route faster.

✔ Is there a better way to follow the black line or check to see if you're still holding the Cargo Box?

✔ Can you use a smaller number in the Counter variable? You might be waiting too long to see if the box has gone into its hole. Beware, though—if you make the number too small, Sweeper might still have the Cargo Box and start turning around anyway, and that would cost you the race.

✔ Park Sweeper. At the end of the race—such as after four or five trips to the Goal Hole—you could make Sweeper go to the Start Circle, turn, and back into the parking garage. You might want to time the race from the moment Sweeper leaves the garage until the instant it stops moving, parked back in its spot.

PROJECT 2

Collision Avoidance Bot

What You'll Need

- ✔ Erector set
- ✔ Erector set motor
- ✔ 12 inches of copper wire (for Grandpa Bumper)
- ✔ Heavy-duty scissors (for Grandpa Bumper)

Time Required

About 3 hours

Difficulty

Easy. You can do this one on your own. If you make Grandpa Bumper or a Bumper from another kind of construction kit, you may need help making the electrical circuit.

2

Project

Using an Erector set, build a simple four-wheeled robot that can respond to collisions by changing direction. You'll build a rover that has a "collision arm" that can change the direction the motor turns when it hits something.

Introduction

Erector sets have been around for longer than I've been alive (which is getting to be a long time), and as a kid I played with them all the time. Armed with an Erector set of metal beams, girders, nuts, and bolts, you could make almost anything. When I was in the 5th grade, I even tried to build a set of human glider wings. That's right. I wanted to make a set of wings long enough to strap to my friend's back, and then Georgie, my gallant volunteer, would use the wings to soar above the ground.

This was a serious project and we planned it in some detail. I knew that the Wright Brothers had made their historic first flights in the early morning because the winds were more favorable at that time of day, so we slated a Saturday morning for the launch of the Erector glider—right after Scooby Doo was over, if I remember correctly. The plan was to make a huge rectangle out of Erector pieces and cover it in plastic wrap (the same stuff you use to put leftovers in the fridge). I painstakingly made a big wing that was about five feet long and a foot or so wide. I then added curved Erector pieces in the middle of the wing. These curved pieces looked like an arch; I made them to sit on Georgie's back. To hold the whole thing in place, I looped twine through some holes and wrapped it around his chest and belly—kind of like a seat belt.

We were lucky to live on a street that had a steep, dirt hill that dropped quite some distance to meet another street down below. Though we lived in the heart of Jersey City, the hill—with patches of grass, an assortment of flowers, and a single, dead tree right in the middle—almost made our little street seem like it was nestled in the woods. We used the hill for sledding in the wintertime and for exploring and adventuring in the summer. Georgie and I assumed that if he got a running start at the top of the hill and jumped right when he reached the edge, he'd quickly soar above the hill and settle gently to the ground in another neighborhood, 50 feet below.

On the fateful Saturday morning, Georgie and I met at the corner and I strapped the Erector wings to his back. He knelt down about ten paces from the edge of the cliff, keeping the wings parallel to the ground. I shouted a short countdown, as if we were launching a rocket. When I reached one and shouted "Blastoff!," Georgie sprinted forward toward the top of the hill. On his second or third step, the wings, too heavy to support their own weight, buckled from the bouncing. They folded around his back like wax wings that got too close to the sun, and Georgie skidded to a stop just short of the edge of the hill.

It's a good thing the wings broke when they did—they'd have surely disintegrated the moment he jumped into the air, and Georgie would have gotten pretty banged up when he came crashing down on the rocks and dirt of the hill.

My glider experiment may not have succeeded, but we can make something almost as cool: an Erector set robot that has a simple collision detection sensor. This sensor—which we'll build from Erector set parts—will help the robot change direction when it bumps into things.

The Robot

Our robot, Bumper, is one of the simplest kinds of semi-autonomous robots (robots that can make decisions on their own). Bumper is a wheeled robot that uses the Erector set motor to toodle around the house. When it touches a wall or the furniture, our mechanical touch sensor will tell the bot to reverse direction. This is an easy bot to build, and I'll tell you how to make two versions of Bumper—a fancy version with a modern Erector set, and a simpler Bumper that uses an old-style Erector set. So whether you have a kit you bought last year or one that has been in the garage for 25 years, you can make Bumper. You can even apply the techniques in this project to make a version of Bumper out of other construction kits, like K'Nex.

The bot itself is the only thing you'll need to make in this project, though you'll want to run it in a big room that gives it a lot of space to change direction.

What's the Difference?

Are old Erector pieces and new Erector pieces very different? You bet! Besides "updating" the motor and battery to make it much easier to use, most of the other parts look quite different, too. Compare the old girder (on the right) to the new girder (on the left):

The Plan

We'll build Bumper (look at Figure 2-1 for a sneak peek at this robot) from a typical Erector set. You don't need anything fancy; almost any kit will do, as long as it includes a motor. I used Erector's **50 Best Of** kit (#9550) to make Bumper, though others like the **30 Best Of** and **40 Best Of** will work just as well.

Figure 2-1
Your Bumper bot will change direction when it runs into an obstacle.

If you have just found an old Erector set kit from the 1960s or 1970s in your garage, you'll find that many of the parts are different—and the directions for Bumper won't work. That's okay—flip to the instructions for Grandpa Bumper (see Figure 2-2), and I'll show you a version of this robot using the older parts.

Once we're done, the robot will drive in a straight line and change direction—drive in reverse, basically—after it hits something. It should be able to change direction every time it hits an object forever, or until the batteries die—whichever comes first.

Building Bumper

Let's begin by making Bumper from a modern set of Erector pieces. There are three main parts to this robot:

✔ Robot chassis
✔ Gearbox
✔ Collision arm

Figure 2-2
You can build
Grandpa Bumper if
you have an older
Erector set.

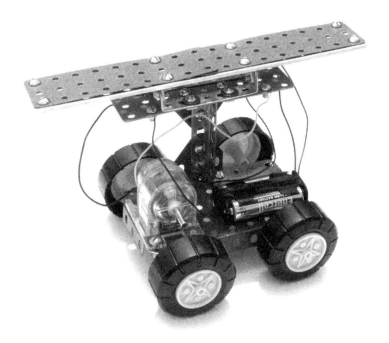

A *chassis* is a simple structure that, in the words of one of my old engineering teachers, "holds the wheels together." The gearbox is a bit more complicated. It is the robot's drive train, and it transfers the power of the motor to the wheels using a collection of interlocking gears.

The great thing about Erector sets today (as opposed to the older ones sold a dozen years ago) is that they now include a fancy gearbox. Instead of connecting the motor to the wheels with a rubber band, you can connect them with an arrangement of gears not entirely unlike the gearbox that's in your car. Most of the construction for Bumper, in fact, will be getting the gearbox built and positioned properly.

In Bumper, the gearbox assembly actually forms a major part of the chassis, so we'll build it all together in one batch of steps.

Finally, we'll make the collision arm. This is the part that makes our creation a robot and not just another Erector car that drives around without any control. More about that later, though—for now, let's get started.

Build the Chassis

If you've already made cars or other sorts of wheeled vehicles with Erectors, nothing here should surprise you. Follow these steps to build Bumper's chassis:

1. If you haven't already done this, assemble the battery case for the motor using the instructions in your Erector set's assembly guidebook.

When done, the switch on the battery case should make the motor run forward or backward (the middle position turns the motor off). We'll need this capability later, when we make the collision arm. The completed battery case should look like this:

2. Take the completed motor/battery case and attach the motor to a gearbox frame. Add a small gear and a clear rubber spacer to the end of the motor's axle. Since our robot drives equally well in both directions, it doesn't really have a "front" or "back"—but we'll consider this gearbox to be the rear anyway.

3. Bolt a second gearbox frame to the first one, and then add a pair of 9X beams to the assembly. These beams will become a key part of the robot chassis, since they'll connect to another gearbox at the front end of the bot.

4. Now it's time to start adding gears. Slide a 50mm axle into the gearbox and add the gears as indicated. You can probably see that as the motor spins, it will turn the large gear which will spin the axle. Soon, we'll add another gear that will connect the small gear outside the gearbox directly to the rear wheel axle.

5. Time to work on the front gearbox. Take another gearbox frame and bolt it to the 9X beams using the large L-brackets. Also add the small L-brackets on top.

6. Now slide a 100mm rod through the two gearboxes, connecting the front and rear ends of the robot, like the transaxle in a car. On each end, place a small gear and a cap. These gears don't do anything yet, but very soon they will transfer power from the motor to the wheels in front.

 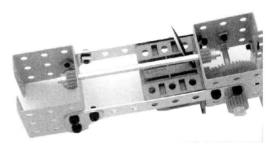

7. Set the robot's chassis aside for a moment and put the wheels together. Push a wheel through a tire, making sure the inside edge of the tire fits around the wheel properly. Repeat this four times, once for each wheel, and then set them aside.

8. Get the robot chassis and turn it upside down, with the rear end closest to you. You'll end up looking at the rear gearbox from the back of the bot. Feed a 130mm axle through the gearbox, inserting a gear and spacer as you go. The gear should contact the small gear that's on the end of the transaxle. Slide three spacers, a wheel gear, and a wheel onto the left end of the axle and cap it with a grommet (it'll be on the right if you're working with the robot upside down). On the other end of the axle, add a small spacer, a gear, a regular spacer, the wheel gear, and the wheel. Hold this all in place with a grommet. The gear you just added to the outside of the gearbox should transfer power from the motor to the rear wheels.

9. Before you go on to the front of the robot and add those wheels, test your bot. Turn on the motor and make sure that the wheels spin; if they don't, make sure the gears line up properly and that there isn't something (like a tight hole) that's keeping the wheels from spinning.

10. Now it's time for the front of the robot. Take two 75mm rods and attach them to their wheels, complete with the spacers and grommets, as shown.

II. Push the right-front wheel through the gearbox, adding the spacer and gear so it connects with the transaxle gear. Add the connector and slide the other wheel into place. You should have a completed gear train, with working front and rear wheels.

I2. Add the grille plate to the front of the robot. The chassis is now complete, but we need a platform for the battery.

I3. Add the large, triangular L-bracket to the front of the robot as shown, complete with a pair of spacers.

14. Build the battery platform using the parts shown here.

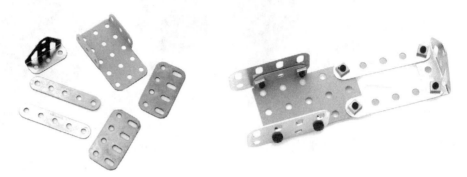

15. Bolt the battery platform to Bumper's chassis by connecting the two L-brackets and then bolting the rear of the platform to the top of the rear-most gearbox.

16. Slide the battery pack under the battery platform but just above the motor. Bolt it to the battery platform from above, as you can see in the following illustration.

17. Create Bumper's antenna array by bolting the angled brackets together, and then attaching it to the top of the battery platform. This part is optional, of course, but I thought this addition made Bumper look a lot more like a lunar rover.

Add the Collision Arm

If you stop now, you'd have an Erector buggy—it'll drive in whatever direction you send it until it hits something, where it would then stop moving (but the motor would keep on trying to push it into the obstacle). We'll build the collision arm next to solve that problem.

I. Attach a narrow 9X beam to a regular 9X beam with a pair of bolts, as shown.

2. Connect an 11X beam to the other end of the narrow beam. Then, take a 15X beam and bolt it to the three-beam assembly with a pair of spacers, centering the beam, as shown here:

3. Take the collision arm and bolt it to the battery pack's power switch with the narrow beam positioned on the "inside" of the battery pack, and the 11X beam pointing toward the back of the bot. Important:

Don't tighten the nut. Leave it slightly loose, or you might tear the switch right off the battery pack. That's it! You've finished Bumper.

Running Bumper

Now that Bumper is complete, it is time to try it out. Bumper works best on a smooth floor, like hard wood or vinyl—it tends to get bogged down on carpet. Point Bumper at a wall or some other obstacle and turn it on by pulling the collision arm forward, toward the front of the robot. The wheels should start spinning; so let it go and watch the action.

Bumper should roll forward. When it gets to an obstacle, Bumper runs right into it—pushing the collision arm backwards, past off, and to the reverse setting. Bumper should immediately roll the other way until it finds an obstacle on the other side of the room. When it gets there, you know what should happen: Bumper's collision arm is pushed back to the forward position, and the robot drives in the direction from whence it came.

It's a very simple idea, but a lot of fun to watch.

How the Collision Arm Works

What's really happening under the hood when the collision arm hits the wall? That's a good question. The switch is simply reversing the polarity of the motor—the direction it spins—by changing the direction of the electrical current that runs through it.

If you have a loose electric motor from another construction kit or model set, you can test this for yourself. Connect the motor to a battery using a pair of wires and pay attention to which way the motor spins. Now, flip the battery around so the negative pole connects to the motor contact that's used to touch the positive pole. The motor should spin in the opposite direction. That's all that happens inside the battery compartment—when the switch is pushed or pulled from one position to the other, the electricity is rerouted, almost as if the battery were turned around, like in our experiment.

If you have an older Erector set, you can build this simple circuit yourself by following the instructions in the section on building Grandpa Bumper.

Building Grandpa Bumper

I call this little guy "Grandpa" even though he looks like a kids' toy because Grandpa Bumper is made from "classic" Erector set pieces—the old kits made before Brio redesigned the sets in the 1990s, and the kind of set you'll find in the garage, basement, and way, way back in the bottom of the toy closet. If you have an old Erector set, Grandpa Bumper is fun to build because we're going to wire the collision arm ourselves, instead of relying on a fancy modern switch to do all the work for us.

Grandpa is very easy to build. You can do most of it in just a few minutes. The chassis is a single part, and serves as the base from which we'll attach the motor and add the collision arm. Let's start with the collision arm support:

1. Bolt two triangle-shaped L-brackets to a 5X girder, as shown:

2. We'll need a few strips of non-metallic material, since we need to insulate several areas of the robot from the flow of electricity. Get a 9×3 plastic plate and bolt it to the triangle bracket.

3. Bolt the entire collision arm support to a 9×5 girder, which will serve as our robot chassis.

4. Now add the motor. Bolt the motor to the end of the girder so its spindle overlooks the second set of holes.

5. Add wheels using a pair of 90mm rods. Before you attach the wheel to the corner of the robot that's directly under the motor, snake a short rubber hand around the motor spindle and the axle. When powered, the motor should transfer power to the wheels through this rubber band. Your Grandpa Bumper should now look more or less like this:

6. Set the robot aside so we can build the collision arm. Attach a pair of small L-brackets to a larger U-shaped bracket (be sure that the bigger bracket is the kind with wide holes, since we'll need to be able to let the bracket slide back and forth around a bolt). Make another set when you are done. Here is what it should look like:

7. Bolt two plastic plates to a pair of 17X beams using four bolts—one at each corner. Don't bother screwing down the middle yet.

8. Bolt the two brackets from step 6 side-by-side to the middle of the 17X beams.

Wire the Collision Circuit

I. Cut two lengths of wire about six inches long and, using a hobby knife, strip about half an inch of insulation off the end. Be careful not to cut the actual copper wire away; you just want to clear away the outer plastic. If you have two different colors, like red and black, it'll be easier to tell them apart.

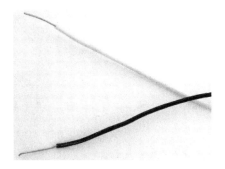

2. Slightly unscrew one of the bolts that's holding the 5X bracket to the collision arm, and wrap the copper end of the wire around the bolt. Retighten the bolt, being careful to keep the wire under the head of the bolt. Do the same thing with the other wire on the neighboring bracket.

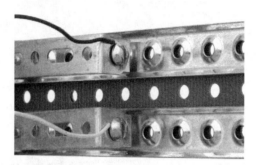

3. Connect those wires to opposite ends of the battery holder and attach the battery holder to the base of the robot, near the motor.

4. That's half of the circuit—to make the robot move, we need to wire the motor to the battery. Cut four more pieces of wire, each about six inches long. Strip off about half an inch of insulation from each end, just like you did in step 1.

5. Attach two of these wires to one of the motor's posts and attach the other two wires (different colors from the first two wires, if possible) to the other motor post. Tighten both posts so the wires won't come off by accident.

6. Add four bolts to the plastic plate on the collision arm, as shown. We're about to make them part of the electric circuit we need to reverse the direction of the robot.

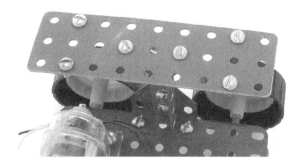

7. Now it's time to attach the four wires from step 5 to the four screws we added to the plate supporting step 6. Take one of the wires and connect it to the nearest bolt on the underside of the plate, where the nut is located. (Loosen the nut, wrap the wire around the screw, and retighten the nut.)

8. Take the other wire that's attached to the same motor post and connect it to the opposite corner—the bolt that is not only six holes away, but also two holes away in the other direction as well. In other words, the two wires from each post should be attached to *diagonally opposite* screws.

9. Using the two wires from the other motor post, wire the two remaining bolts on the collision arm plate.

10. Now it's time to do a little test. The circuit is live and waiting for a connection so the motor can start running. Take the collision arm and touch its brackets to the two bolts at the motor end of the robot. Does it try to roll in that direction, so the motor is at the front of the robot, or does it try to roll away, making the motor at the back? If the motor is at the front, you're in business. Go on to step 10. But if the robot rolled the wrong way, reverse the two battery wires, switching them to opposite brackets.

11. So that the motor doesn't start every time we accidentally complete the circuit, temporarily disconnect one of the battery wires.

12. Finally, it's time to connect the collision arm. Take two bolts and attach it to the plastic collision arm support. Use washers if you have them, and don't tighten the nuts to the bolts—leave them slightly loose, so the arm can slide back and forth.

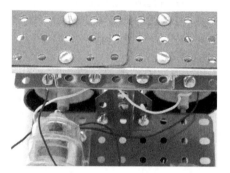

Running Grandpa Bumper

Grandpa Bumper works just like Bumper—set it on a flat, smooth floor and point it at a wall or some other obstacle. When you're ready to start, make sure the collision arm is in a "neutral" position (not touching either set of bolts) and reattach the loose wire. When the wire is connected, tap the collision arm forward and the robot should roll forward, hit the obstacle, and change direction.

The reason that Grandpa Bumper works is that you created a circuit that gives the electricity two possible paths through the motor. If you trace the path through the wires you rigged up to the collision arm, you'll see that the electricity moves in one direction when the robot moves forward (clockwise, perhaps), but has to take the opposite route (counterclockwise) when the arm touches the other bolts.

Improving Bumper

Hopefully, Bumper and Grandpa Bumper worked for you right away. You may have noticed some problems, though, that an ingenious roboticist like yourself might want to solve:

✔ Bumper doesn't always hit the obstacle with the collision arm. If Bumper hits a narrow or short obstacle that the arm can't reach, the robot tries to keep driving until you come over and rescue it. Can you modify the collision arm so that it stands a better chance of feeling all the collisions Bumper might have?

✔ Bumper only goes in a straight line. How hard would it be to put one set of wheels on a swivel so that it turns in unpredictable directions? Is it possible to design the robot so it only turns after changing directions? How? (Hint: Consider putting a "swivel" assembly on just one set of wheels. Which wheels would get the swivel?)

✔ If you built Grandpa Bumper, you may have found that the collision arm requires frequent adjustment. Is there a better way to let the arm move back and forth, without relying on loose bolts?

✔ Can you make Bumper run better on a variety of floor surfaces? Would changing the wheels affect drivability on rugs?

✔ Since Grandpa Bumper doesn't have a power switch, you have to constantly connect and disconnect a wire to get it to work. Can you use Erector pieces to add your own switch to the robot?

Other Bumpers

In this project, you've seen how to make two different variations on a collision-avoidance robot—one with a sealed switch that we pushed around with a collision arm, and another with a collision circuit that we made ourselves out of just six pieces of wire. Hopefully, that'll give you some ideas about other robots you can make. You can make your own version of Bumper from K'Nex pieces, for instance, as well as old model kits or balsa wood and spare parts from Radio Shack. If you have an old motor and battery case lying around that you don't mind performing surgery on, you can cut the wire that connects the battery case and motor. Once they're disconnected, you can rig a collision circuit yourself on almost anything that moves.

PROJECT 3

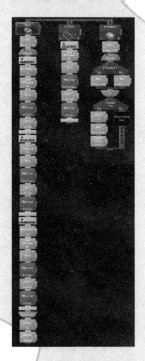

MindStorms Combat Robots

What You'll Need

Lego MindStorms Robotic Invention System 2.0. You can use an older MindStorms kit, but some of the directions will not match, and you'll have to improvise.

- ✔ One or two foam boards, at least 32×40 inches
- ✔ Electrical tape (½-inch wide)
- ✔ Pencil
- ✔ Scissors

Time Required

About 8 hours

Difficulty

Challenging. You may need some help, especially when it comes to attaching the hammer and fine-tuning the programming to work with your bot.

Project

Construct a combat robot from a Lego MindStorms kit and program it to battle another robot in a "combat arena." The robot will have a kill hammer that swings up and down to hit the other robot. Since the hammer will have a touch sensor built in, it will record "kills." We'll program the robots to fight until a specific score is reached, such as "5 hammer kills."

Introduction

You probably already know that robots that beat each other up have become very popular. For a long time, the only place you could see robot combat was in a Rock 'em Sock 'em Robots tabletop game, or one of those old Japanese monster movies in which a robot version of Godzilla had to fight a giant robot shaped like a guy in a robot suit.

Rock 'em Sock 'em Robots were great. You played against a friend and controlled your plastic robot boxer with a pair of controls that stuck out of the side of the boxing ring. The goal was to knock the other robot's head off with a robotic uppercut.

These days, you can find robot combat on TV just by flipping a few channels. So instead of Rock 'em Sock 'em Robots, you get to see robots with names like *Diesector* and *Overkill* beating on each other with hammers and saw blades.

In this project, we're going to build something like a cross between Rock 'em Sock 'em Robots and BattleBots. But instead of fighting by remote control, we're going to equip our robot with the ability to fight on its own. Then, we'll turn two of them loose and watch the mayhem!

The Robot

Say hello to Thor in Figure 3-1. Thor is a killing machine designed to pound your opponent into oblivion. It won't stop until there's nothing left of your enemy but...

Figure 3-1
Thor's hammer has a touch sensor so it knows when it hits other robots.

Actually, Thor won't be quite that destructive. I've named him Thor because Thor is the name of a mythical god who used lightning like a giant hammer. Our robot Thor has a hammer too—kind of like the hammer weapons you see in robot combat on television. Rather than beat the opposing robot to death, though, our robot will be equipped with a touch sensor at the end of the hammer, and each time it manages to touch the opposing robot, it'll score a point. The robot with the most points wins!

Like the book's first robot project, we'll make Thor with Lego MindStorms. We'll need two robots for full-up robot-on-robot combat, so get a friend to build a Thor as well. If you only have one MindStorms set available, you can test the hammer with non-moving Lego structures. Unfortunately, though, they won't be able to fight back.

The robots will fight inside an arena like the one in Figure 3-2. In fact, they'll be able to go anywhere they like, as long as they stay inside the combat area, which we'll create by making a black outline around the edges of a big piece of foam board. The robots will move around on their own, dropping their hammers according to their programming. When they hit something, they'll beep to let you know a hit was scored. The robots will also keep track of their scores on their LCD displays, and the first bot to reach the winning score will stop to announce the win.

Figure 3-2
Your arena should
be big enough that
the robots have
room to move
around.

Thor will be unique—and not just because it's a combat robot. You'll see that we're making the robot move and turn with just one motor—if you couldn't quite figure out how to build the "top secret" one-motor bot at the end of the Lego MindStorms manual, that's okay—we'll go through it step-by-step in this project. We need to drive the robot with just one motor, because we need a second motor to run the hammer. The robot will also have a light sensor for staying inside the arena, and it'll let you know what it's up to with both sound and the LCD display. Since there's a tremendous amount of force involved in raising and lowering the hammer, Thor is built like a tank—it's probably the most rugged MindStorms robot you'll ever build.

The Plan

We'll build Thor using a standard set of Lego MindStorms and then program it using the MindStorms programming language. The arena will be built from a large foam board (or some other large, white surface). After everything is built, it's time for combat. You can only make one robot with a MindStorms kit, so you'll need a friend to build a Thor as well if you want to compete.

Building Thor

Thor is really made from just three major parts: the driving base, the light sensor, and the hammer. We'll start by building the driving base, which is actually the most complex part of the robot. It uses special gears and gadgets to turn whenever the bot drives backward.

Build the Driving Base

Here's how to make the base of our combat robot:

1. To make the base, start by adding the appropriate connectors to the 16X beam. Specifically, push an 8X rod through the fourth hole and hold it in place with a small gear and a spacer. Add the 2X flat blocks (one of the blocks has a flange that will eventually help hold a motor in place).

2. Add the angled gear assembly. The angled gears may look complicated, but they let the two front wheels turn independently. As you'll see, when the motor spins, the angled gears turn both wheels. But if one of the wheels doesn't turn for some reason (and we'll provide that reason later when we make the gear lock), the other wheel spins just fine anyway. To start making the angled gears, place an angled gear in the middle of the double gear housing. Push a 6X rod into the beam's second hole, into the double gear housing, and into the small angled gear that meshes with the middle gear. The rod should go halfway through the double gear housing. Lock it in place by putting a gear on the other side of the beam.

3. Continue building the angled gear assembly by pushing a 6X rod into the double gear housing from the other side, snagging the last angled gear in the process.

4. Build the gear lock assembly from a 4X rod and the other parts in the picture. See "How Does the Gear Lock Work?" later in the chapter for an explanation of what this gadget will do.

5. Snap the gear lock assembly into place on the beam.

6. Snap another flanged block into place on the bottom of the beam, right under the flanged block that's already there. Place the motor in position (the flange on the flat blocks should help guide the motor into the right position) and add a power cable. Add the blocks, as shown. These hold the motor in place and help build up the base so it can be attached securely to the RCX controller. Add a big gear to the motor's spindle.

7. Now it's time to add the other half of the driving base. Take another 16X beam and 3X rod and add the connectors and gears pictured here.

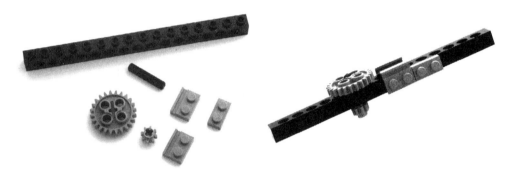

8. Slide the second beam onto the rest of the driving base and lock it in place with more blocks on the motor and the pair of spacers on the front wheel axle.

9. We've almost got a working drive train! Add a big gear to complete the transfer of power from the motor to the front wheels. Once you do that, you should be able to turn the motor and watch the front wheels spin.

10. If all that went well, add the wheels. Slide the large, rubber wheels onto the front axle, using a spacer between the gear and the wheel on the front right side. Then, slip an 8X rod to the rear of the drive, positioning a small wheel between the beams first. Center the wheel and add a pair of spacers to the outside of the beams to hold it in place.

11. Build up the back of the driving base with the additional blocks, as shown.

12. Attach the blue connector to two 16X beams.

13. Press your new assembly into the top of the driving base you've already made, putting the blue connector up front and the back of the beams flush with the rear of the robot.

14. Snap the RCX controller onto the top of the beams so it's flush with the back of the driving base. Plug the motor into power port C.

That's the driving base—it's ready to roll. You can test the backup-and-turn feature now if you want to by writing a short program that makes it go forward and backward. When you're happy with the way it works, set it aside so you can work on the other parts of the robot. Here's what Thor should look like so far:

How Does the Gear Lock Work?

The gear lock is the gadget that will let the robot turn whenever it moves backward. It's a clever way to both move and turn using just a single motor. But what does it do?

Check out the gear lock mechanism by holding the driving base upright. Spin the motor and you should see the motor's gear turn the nearby gear, which turns other gears and so on... until the front axle spins, turning the wheels.

If you turn the motor so that the wheels spin forward, you should see the gear lock bounce along happily on top of the gear's teeth. It might make a little clacking sound (like when you stick a card in the spokes of a bike), but it doesn't interfere with the way the wheels turn.

Now, turn the motor the other direction, so it makes the front wheels spin backward. Do you see the difference? One wheel still spins just fine, but the wheel near the gear lock can't turn because the gear lock has literally jammed itself in between the teeth of the gear. The robot will turn, since only one wheel is spinning. As soon as you roll forward again, the gear lock will let the wheel turn freely again.

Build the Light Sensor

After all that hard work, let's make something easy—the light sensor. The light sensor is a snap to assemble:

I. Push a 4X rod through a pair of 2×1 blocks.

2. Push two connectors into each side of a blue connector block.

3. Combine the two assemblies with a pair of L-brackets.

4. Attach your light sensor to the 2×1 blocks and attach the entire light sensor assembly to the front of Thor using a yellow double connector. Finally, plug the light sensor into port 1. That's it!

Make Thor's Hammer

If you were a Norse god, getting a supernatural hammer would probably be the easy part. The hard part? Controlling it. After all, your hammer would be big, heavy, and more powerful than a locomotive. You'd have to work out to stay in shape at a special gym for gods so you could wield it safely, and you'd have to keep it in a special god-like hammer carrying case. The same thing is true for our little Thor—building the hammer itself is easy. Attaching it to the robot so Thor doesn't tear itself apart every time the hammer flies is the important part.

In addition to worrying about holding all this together, the hammer has two important parts: the motor, which swings it up and down, and a touch sensor. Why a touch sensor? Well, since we're not really hacking the other robot to bits, we need some way to know when we've won. The touch sensor, at the very end of the hammer, lets us know when we touch our opponent.

Let's get started:

I. We'll begin by making the motor assembly. It's the "stand" that the hammer will be attached to. Snap a pair of 4×1 thin blocks under the motor, around the bulge, so it can sit flat. Lay two 8×2 thin blocks on the table and position the motor on top, as shown. Press the connecting wire onto the motor and carefully lay the wire through the small wire channel on the top of the motor. Add a medium-sized gear to the motor spindle.

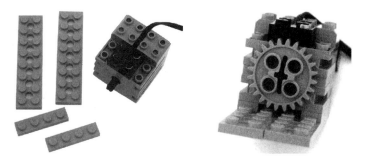

2. Build a tower of four 4×2 blocks on the other end of the base. On top of that, add a thin 4×2 block and two 4×1 blocks with holes. Eventually, this will hold the hammer's axle in position.

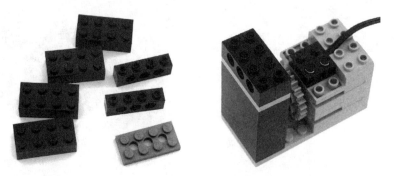

3. Add two more 4×1 blocks with holes to the top of the motor. Be careful that the wire is down in its channel, or it'll keep these two blocks from staying where they belong on top of the motor.

4. Snap a 2×1 and two thin 2×1 blocks on top of the motor in front of the power block. When the hammer comes crashing down in combat, this block keeps the hammer from falling too far and striking the arena floor. After you've finished the motor assembly; set it aside for a few minutes so we can build the hammer itself.

5. Let's continue with the "business end" of the hammer—the part that other robots should be afraid of. Take two 4X rods and push them into the angled connectors, as shown. Using another 4X rod, attach the connectors on either side of the black L-bracket. Cap them with small spacers. Then, push a pair of long spacers into place on the rods and add "bumpers" to the end of the rods. Put it aside for a moment.

6. Push two 3X rods through an oval block, as shown, leaving just a little of each rod sticking out of the oval.

7. Attach a wire block to the touch sensor. Then push a spacer onto the rod at the fat end of the oval. Push the touch sensor onto the other rod and hold it there with another spacer.

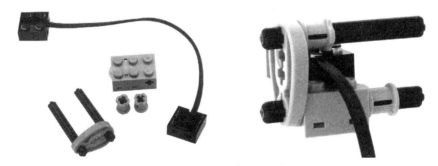

8. Slide the end of the black L-bracket from step 5 onto the rod at the fat end of the oval. You should now be able to tap the bumper to activate the touch sensor.

9. Take a long yellow bumper piece and slide it onto the rod next to the black L-bracket, as shown, and cap it with another oval. You've finished the end of the hammer, but right now it's so short that we'll just end up beating on our own robot. Thor needs a long "arm" so we can strike at other robots.

10. Find two 16X beams and push a connector with a star-shaped end into the second hole of one of them so the star pattern sticks out. Press a large gear into the star connector so the gear's center hole is in line with the beam's first hole. When the motor turns the gear, this connector will force the hammer to turn at the same time.

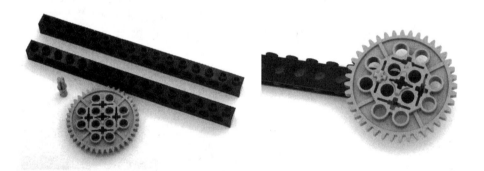

11. Attach the pair of 16X beams to the yellow bumper with long black connectors. The connectors go through one of the black beams, through the yellow bumper in the middle, and out the other side to attach to the other beam.

12. It's show time. Get the motor assembly and slide a 12X rod through the middle hole of the top block. Position the hammer assembly over the motor so the gears line up and then continue pushing the rod until it goes through the first hole of the 16X beams and the center hole of the gear. Push the rod until it comes out of the top block on the other side. Carefully, set it aside for a moment.

13. Attach three 2×2 blocks and a 4×2 block to the top of the drive base right in front of the RCX controller, building up the bottom around the blue connector.

14. Very carefully, press the motor and hammer assembly onto the blocks you just added in the last step.

15. It would take an act of Thor (the mythical one, not the robot) to keep the hammer attached to your robot for more than a few seconds of actual operation when it's assembled like this. We need to reinforce it.

For starters, connect two 8X beams to the top of the hammer assembly, pointed toward the back of the robot. Add a 4X beam to the bottom of the motor.

16. Using a 10X beam and a pair of connectors, secure the beam on the top of the motor to the beam on the bottom of the motor. We'll reinforce the other side with a different sort of beam arrangement.

17. Push a 12X rod through the beam directly under the RCX controller. Use the fifth hole from the rear of the robot. Attach a connector into the first hole of a 12X beam and push the connector into the last hole of the beam on top of the hammer assembly. At the same time, push the other end of the beam through the 12X rod. Don't worry—the rod really should be at an angle.

18. Repeat the process with another 12X beam and connector on the other side of the robot. Then, cap the exposed ends of the rod with spacers.

19. Drive a 10X rod through the beams under the RCX controller. Use hole number 8 if you count from the rear of the robot. Use another 12X beam to connect this rod to the rod that goes through the hammer's big gear. Cap the lower rod with spacers at both ends.

20. We just have one more reinforcement to go. Reinforce the top of the hammer assembly with a pair of 8X beams, and put two 4×2 blocks in the middle of the structure. Not only do these blocks help hold things together, but they also limit how far back the hammer can go—the motor will thank you for it.

21. Finally, connect the touch sensor's wire to port 3. The touch sensor won't reach, so you need to extend the wire with a spare wire. You can attach the blocks to one of the hammer's beams, as shown here:

22. Test your assembly by moving the hammer up and down with your hand. You should see that the two gears connect, so the motor turns when you move the hammer. The hammer should also have limits on how far up and down it can go. If everything looks good, congratulations—you're done!

Making the Arena

Thor is ready for some action, but we need a combat arena for it to operate in. It would be great if we could program our robots to run around a huge stadium, but we'll have to be content with a playfield that fits in the living room—so let's use some big slabs of foam board or poster board from a hobby store.

How will Thor know where to find the edges of the arena? The easiest way is to mark the edges of the combat zone with a thick black line. The light sensor can tell Thor it has reached the edge, and that's when Thor will back up and turn to stay inside.

Our arena doesn't have to be fancy; a big rectangle just a little smaller than the foam board will do. Choose the biggest piece of foam board you can get your hands on (I used one that measured 32×40 inches) and lightly draw on the board where the tape will go (such as two inches in from the edge of the board). Then, lay out four lengths of ½-inch-wide black electrical tape over your sketch, making a big rectangle on your board. As you can see here, I rounded the corners of my arena a bit:

If you'd like to, make the arena even bigger. Instead of laying the tape around one board, place two 32×40-inch foam boards side-by-side and create a huge rectangle that spans both boards. To do that, have someone help you by holding the two boards firmly together so there's no space between their edges. Then, apply one long piece of electrical tape across them. Not only will you end up with a big arena, but the tape that forms the outline of the arena will help hold the boards together for you. If you really want them to stay together, though, flip the boards over and add more tape there.

Programming Thor

Thor may be finished, but right now it's not very smart. In fact, all it knows how to do is sit around and stare at you. What Thor really wants to do is drive around and pound on other robots, but we need to teach it how to do that with some programming. Remember, unlike a BattleBot, Thor will use its programming to work on its own. It doesn't need a human to operate it.

Envision the Program

If you've already built Project 1, you know the drill: it's time to use the Lego MindStorms software to program our robot. But before we get there, let's decide exactly what we expect Thor to do. Put Thor inside the arena and put in another object—a few Lego blocks, maybe—that we can pretend is the other robot. Here's what we can do with Thor:

1. Begin by raising the hammer. This will get Thor ready to attack.

2. We now want to look for the other robot. But how can we do that? We don't really have a way to find other robots, so we're going to have to move around the arena randomly. Let's tell Thor to move forward some random distance.

3. Is the robot in front of us? We don't know for sure—but let's drop the hammer just in case.

4. After waiting a moment, let's haul the hammer up so it's ready to attack again.

5. Move around some more and drop the hammer again.

You get the idea. Let's just do that over and over.

But wait—what's that you say? We need to stay inside the arena? Good point! We should also check constantly for the black line that will tell us we're about to cross out of the combat zone. If we find ourselves crossing the edge of the arena, we'll back up—which will also make us turn. That way, we'll head off in a different direction when we go forward again.

We'll also add some other doodads to the program. Each time we score a hit, for instance, Thor will beep at us and keep track of its own score. When Thor reaches a certain number of "kills," it'll automatically stop and tell us it has won the game.

See? Piece of cake! Let's get started.

Thor's Dance

Let's start with Thor's basic moves—what you might call his "dance". You know, he lifts his hammer, he moves, then he drops the hammer in hopes of poking another robot. Then he does it all over again. In fact, since Thor is performing three tasks in the dance, I put them into three individual subroutines, as you can see here:

Each "subroutine" is actually a bunch of separate commands. But by combining them into one block and giving them a special name, I've made the program look a lot neater.

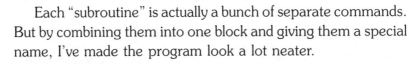

What's a Small Block?

In this project, we use a lot of Small Blocks to program Thor. You might not realize that the Big Blocks you use to program your robots—with commands like Move, Turn, and Spin—are really made up of a lot of Small Blocks that do all the hard work, like turning on the right power port and setting the direction that the motors turn. Since Thor has a lot of special features that the Big Blocks can't handle, we'll be programming this guy mainly with Small Blocks.

Start by raising the hammer. For this, we'll need to use MindStorms Small Blocks. The Big Blocks make it easy to tell the robot to do common tasks, like drive forward or turn. But there's no Big Block for "lift the hammer," so let's do it ourselves with Small Blocks instead.

1. Every time we move the hammer around, we should be just a little worried about throwing the hammer around too hard and too fast. The hammer is big and heavy, and if we're too rough, we might tear Thor apart. So the first thing we want to do is slow down the speed at which the motor runs. Click the Small Blocks button, then open the Power blocks and add the Set Power block to the program. The motor's maximum power is 8, so let's open the block and change the power level for power port A to 6.

2. Next, set the motor's direction with a Set Direction block. The hammer motor is attached to power port A, so adjust this block to A and click on the down direction. As long as you attached Thor's power blocks correctly, that will pull the hammer up. (If you test the program and this step doesn't work correctly because the motor is turning the wrong way, just set the direction to up instead.)

3. Now we want to turn the motor on. Drag the On box to the program and set it so only port A is on.

4. How long should it run? That's a good question—it depends on your particular robot, but I found that my Thor needed about 1.2 seconds to get the hammer upright. Click the Wait button and drag a Wait For box to the program. Wait for 1.2 seconds, then turn the motor off with an old-fashioned Off box (from the Power section of the Small Boxes). Only turn port A off, since that's the one with the hammer motor. All together, it should look like this:

5. Feel free to test your bot and fine-tune the hammer. When you're ready, you might want to create your own custom block for these steps to make the program easier to follow. Click My Blocks and choose Create a New Block. Name it something you'll remember— like HammerUp—and drag the steps you just made into it.

6. Now it's time to move the bot. These steps will look similar to the hammer routine. Start by setting the direction of the motor (set port C to down) and then turn on the motor with an On block set just to port C.

7. How long should Thor drive forward? Let's make it a random amount of time—that way the bot is guaranteed to explore new and different parts of the arena all the time. The command to use is Wait For (from the Wait blocks). When you open the block, choose Random from the menu and then tell it to run for any time between 2 and 4 seconds. The exact time you configure is up to you, but try these settings for now.

8. Finally, turn off the motor at port C and add a Wait For 1 second block.

9. Create a new My Block called MoveThor and copy all of these steps into it.

10. The dance is almost over—now it's time to drop the hammer after waiting a polite 1 second in our new position. For our final subroutine, called HammerDown, let's set the power level low to control the speed at which the hammer drops. Set the Power for port A to 4 and then set the direction to up—exactly the opposite from when you raised it back at the beginning of the program. You may need to experiment with the proper timing, but my Thor worked well with a Wait For of about .7 seconds. Then, turn port A off and wait for a second or so before doing anything else.

II. Put all of those commands inside a Repeat box that's set to run two or three times, and test your newly programmed Thor. It should lift the hammer, drive a short distance, and drop the hammer. After a short pause, it should lift the hammer and do it all over again.

Stay in the Arena

How are we doing? If Thor is working the way you expect, it's time to start adding the other parts of the program. It might be handy to keep Thor inside the arena even during testing, so let's add that section of the program next.

I. This is really, really easy. From the Sensors box, drag a Light Sensor onto the program. We want to back up anytime we cross the black line, so set it to If Dark, configure it for port 1, where we plugged in the light sensor, and leave the other settings alone. Notice that the If Dark box is hanging off by itself on the side of the program; anytime Thor sees a dark line, it'll perform whatever commands are under this box.

2. Let's create a My Block called BackThor. In it, we'll put all the commands we need to move backward.

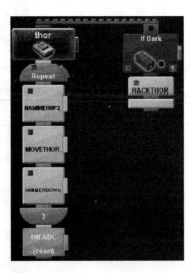

3. I think you'll find that we need to add the same blocks as in the MoveThor commands, only change the direction of the motor. Be

sure to set the direction at port C, turn it on, and wait a few random seconds. Then, turn the motor off and wait a second before we jump into the next step. It looks like this:

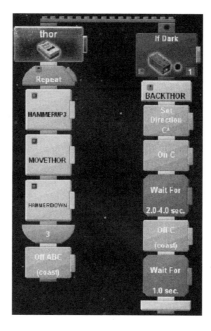

4. Test your bot to make sure everything is still working the way you expect.

Keep Score

We're almost done. All that's left is to actually keep score. We can do that with the same sort of sensor block we just used to check for the boundary of the arena:

1. Drag a Touch Sensor block from the Sensors to the program. Set it to check port 3 to see if it has been pressed—if it has, we want to beep and keep track of the score. We'll do that in the next few steps.

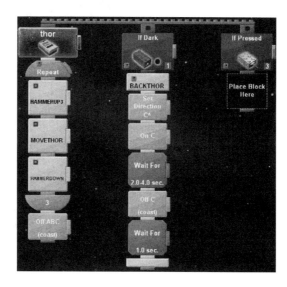

2. The first thing we should do when we touch the other robot is beep. We're winning, so let's make some noise! Go back to the Small Blocks and look for Sound. Drag the Beep block to the program and set it to beep three times.

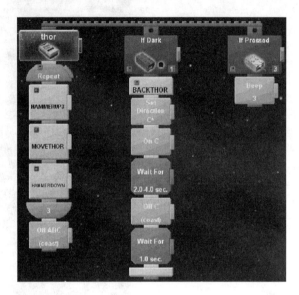

3. We can keep score with a variable—that's just a placeholder that represents the score. We can program Thor to change the value of the variable every time it hits the opponent. In Small Blocks, look for Variables and drag Set to the program—place it right at the start of the program, above the Repeat block for Thor's dance. Open the block and, in the menu, choose Create New Variable. Name this variable Score. Set it to zero, since the game just started and the score should be zero.

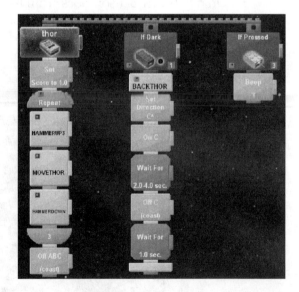

4. Now drag the Add block to the program under the Beep block. Set it so it adds one to the score.

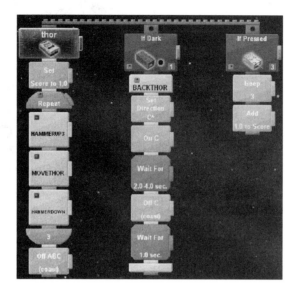

5. We also want to display that score on the RCX controller's LCD screen. You'll be able to look at your robot anytime it is in the arena during battle and see what the score is. To do that, look for Comm (that's short for communications) in the Small Blocks and add Display Value to the program—make it display (you guessed it) Score.

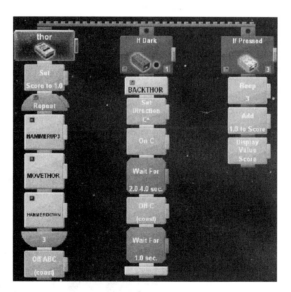

6. Finally, let's change the Repeat block around Thor's dance. Instead of just repeating the dance a few times, add the Repeat Until block to the program and set it so it repeats until Score is 4. That way, the robot will stop competing as soon as it scores 4 kills. After the Repeat Until block, add an Off block to shut the robot's motors down, and—just for the heck of it—play a string of victory beeps.

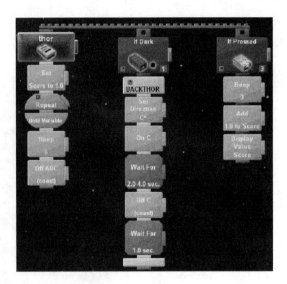

Fine-Tune Thor

Go ahead and test your program. You'll probably find a small problem with the program—Thor registers a "hit" every time the hammer goes up or comes down. You may have even guessed that would happen the first time you saw the hammer slam up or down like a miniature steam shovel. Well, there's an easy way to solve this little dilemma. We just assume that if we hit a real target, the hit will register for more than a split second—so we test for a hit three times very quickly. If the hammer's touch sensor stays on long enough to pass the test, it's a valid point. Here's what you can do:

1. Under the If Pressed block, add a Repeat For block and set it to 3. Whatever we put in here will happen three times.

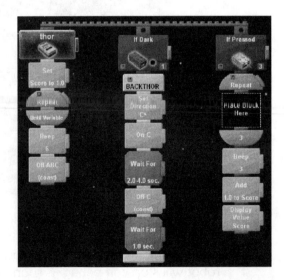

2. In the Repeat For block, add a Yes or No block. Configure it to look for touch on Port 2. If it's pressed, add one to a variable named Press.

88

If Pressed is No, reset the variable called Press to zero. Do you see what happens here? If the touch sensor is pressed, it checks three more times. Each time it checks, if the sensor is still pressed, it adds one to a variable called Press. If it's ever not pressed during those three checks, the variable is set to zero.

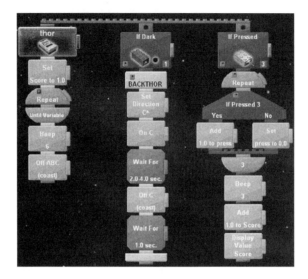

3. Add a Yes or No block under the Repeat block, and configure it for "If Press = 3." Whatever is under the Yes side will happen if Press is 3. Place all the good stuff—like the beep, scoring, and display commands— under Yes. Leave No empty. Finally, add a block above the Repeat block that sets the variable Press to 0.

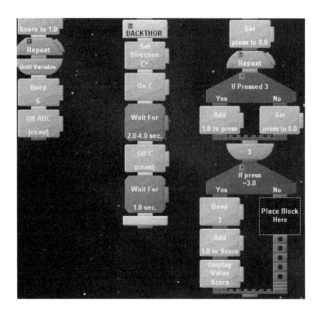

That's the entire program. The whole thing looks something like Figure 3-3.

Figure 3-3
The entire Thor
program

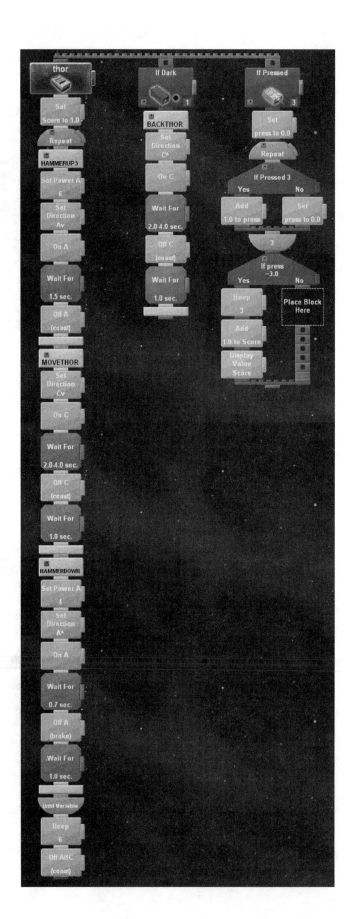

Now you should be able to take two Thors, put them in the arena, and let them battle. The first one to reach four kills wins.

Improving Thor

Thor is now a mighty killing machine. But what else can you do to make it better? Try some of these special projects:

✔ Try to make Thor play a different sound (or a different number of sounds) for each kill, so you don't have to look at the display to know how well it is doing.

✔ To minimize the risk of collisions, make Thor back up a little after each good kill.

✔ Add a touch sensor and a bumper to the front of Thor's body, right in front of or on top of the light sensor. Only drop the hammer when you actually touch the other robot by driving into it with your bumper.

✔ Add a touch sensor to the top or rear of the robot. Change the rules (and the program) so that hitting that one special spot is like catching the snitch in Quiddich—an automatic win for the other robot.

✔ Experiment with ways of moving forward and backward. Is there a way to move around the arena that makes you have better luck at hitting the enemy robot?

PROJECT 4

Your Own Mars Pathfinder

What You'll Need

- ✔ A large D- or E-engine model rocket kit with a diameter around 4 inches
- ✔ Model rocket supplies, like a launch pad, controller, motors and igniters, and wadding
- ✔ $\frac{3}{32}$ × 3-inch sheet of balsa wood
- ✔ Pinewood derby-style racing wheels
- ✔ Thin brass rod (a common model-building supply available at most hobby and craft stores)
- ✔ Five-minute epoxy
- ✔ Masking tape
- ✔ Double-sided, foam-backed tape
- ✔ Solar array (available at most hobby and electronics stores—about .5 amp)
- ✔ Small motor (also available from hobby and electronics stores)
- ✔ Model rocket recovery cable (parachute clips connected by short metal wire, such as ones made by Rhino Cable)
- ✔ 18- or 24-inch model rocket parachute
- ✔ Modeling supplies, such as a hobby knife, scissors, pliers, and ruler
- ✔ Drill and drill bits

Time Required

About 25 hours

Difficulty

Complicated. Your dad or mom will probably need to help.

4

Project

Build a four-wheeled, solar-powered rover and a model rocket. Launch the rover inside the rocket so that the rover lands intact, separates from its parachute, and drives away under its own power.

Introduction

One of the most exciting uses for robots is in the exploration of space. NASA and other space exploration agencies routinely send robots into space to explore the cosmos. Why do they use robots? The most important reason is that it's a lot cheaper and safer than sending people into space.

Robots are great for handling routine stuff, like flying past a planet and taking pictures. Robots aren't so good at dealing with problems like stuck valves, broken cameras, misfiring rocket engines, and that sort of thing. That's why NASA sent human beings to the Moon—starting with Apollo 11 in 1969, 12 humans managed to visit the Moon. Those people collected rock and dirt samples, took lots of pictures, experimented in low gravity, and played golf, among other things. No one has sent humans to another world since the last Apollo mission in 1973, but the United States and Russia are both interested in sending humans to Mars sometime in the next 15 or 20 years—and we might even do it together, as a joint U.S.-Russian trip. That's pretty exciting.

In the meantime, we rely on robots. And robots are getting better at exploring space. In fact, one of the most successful space robot missions in the history of NASA was a mission to Mars called Pathfinder. In 1997, the Pathfinder mission went to Mars to explore the "Red Planet." What was unique about Pathfinder was the fact that the mission included a rover—a four-wheeled, solar-powered robot that could move around the planet and explore hundreds of yards away from the main landing craft.

The rover, seen in Figure 4-1, was called Sojourner, and it was shaped kind of like a skateboard, with a long, flat top made completely from solar cells (that's how it got its power), and was about five feet long. Sojourner traveled millions of miles inside a rocket to reach Mars, then it entered the Martian atmosphere and plummeted at extremely high speed towards the surface. Throughout the descent, a heat shield protected the robot from the extremely high temperatures of re-entry.

Figure 4-1
Sojourner wheeled around Mars, looking for rocks to sample.

About 300 yards above the surface, though, NASA engineers made something interesting happen. Sojourner's airbags inflated. After that, the robot was totally surrounded by what looked like huge balloons, or perhaps beach balls in a big net. When the bot hit the Martian surface, the airbags absorbed the impact and protected the robot. It bounced around on the surface of Mars for miles, until finally coming to rest.

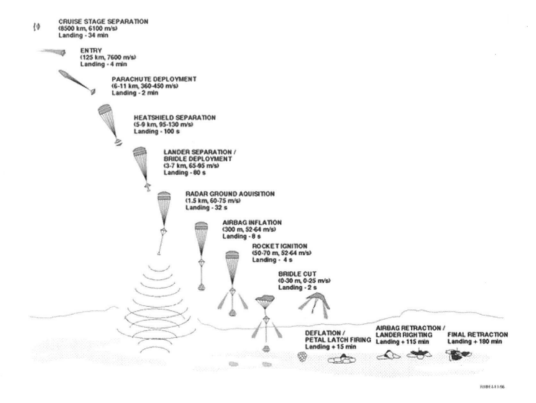

Finally, the lander opened up, pushing the airbags out of the way, and Sojourner drove off to prove that rover-like robots can help us explore space.

If you want to learn more about Pathfinder, see lots of cool pictures, and even look at videos and animations of the robot in action, visit some of these web sites:

- ✔ http://mars.jpl.nasa.gov/
- ✔ http://science.ksc.nasa.gov/mars/vrml/vrml.html
- ✔ http://mars.jpl.nasa.gov/MPF/mpf/rover.html
- ✔ http://mars.jpl.nasa.gov/MPF/mpf/mission.html

The Robot

That's what we're going to do in this project—try to make a bot that's like the Mars Pathfinder mission. Our Little Sojourner is a simple three-wheeled Rover that looks sort of like the Sojourner that visited Mars in 1997. (You can see our homemade version in Figure 4-2.) Little Sojourner is a working solar-powered rover; the solar cells don't generate a ton of power, but on a sunny day they can move the robot around quite nicely on a smooth, flat surface. We'll use three wheels instead of four so we can attach the front wheel directly to the motor in the middle of the body.

Figure 4-2
Little Sojourner is a working solar-powered rover.

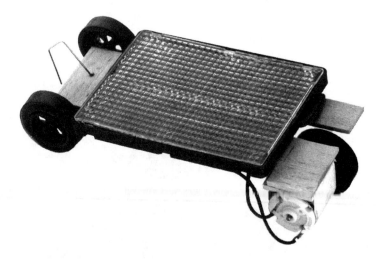

The rover is just part of this project, though. If you want to see this project all the way through, you'll need to build a model rocket and launch Little Sojourner. If all goes well, the bot will ascend with the rocket and then pop out of the rocket body at the same time that the rocket's parachute deploys. Little Sojourner has its own parachute, which it'll use to slowly return to earth. When it reaches the surface, the parachute should slip away from the robot and the robot will slowly drive away.

Sound complicated? It is, a bit. There's a lot that can go wrong during this launch sequence, so don't be surprised if you have to launch it a few times before it works properly. It's true that Mars Pathfinder worked almost flawlessly for NASA, but a lot of other robots failed in their Martian missions as well. So if you get Little Sojourner to work correctly, consider yourself an unofficial rocket scientist!

The Plan

As you can see from the "What You'll Need" list, we're going to make this project more or less from scratch—we're not using Legos or Erectors or anything like that. Make a trip to your local hobby or craft store and stock up on supplies like the balsa wood, motor, and solar cell. We'll start by building the model rocket. Why? We'll need the rocket so we know how large the robot can be. After it's done, we'll then build and test the robot. As you'll see, we can test the robot without launching it. That's a good thing, since you may need to make changes to the robot before it finds itself 300 feet in the air.

Building Little Pathfinder

If the rover bot is called Little Sojourner, that would make the rocket Little Pathfinder. This part I'll leave mostly up to you. The model rocket is an optional part of this project, but trust me: it's really cool when all the parts come together and Little Sojourner drives off after having just blasted a few hundred feet into the air. You don't have to build any specific rocket model kit, but I highly recommend building the largest, fattest rocket you can get your hands on. I've tested Little Sojourner in these two rocket kits:

- ✔ Estes V-2
- ✔ Estes Pershing

Both have a 4-inch body tube diameter, which is about the biggest rocket body you can buy in a kit. That's just about right for our Little Sojourner. If you build your model rocket in the ordinary way, you probably won't have to make any adjustments for the robot unless the solar array is large (see the next section, "Adjust your Rocket Kit," for details).

If you've never made a model rocket before, you should get some help. A large rocket is no harder to build that a smaller model rocket, but there are a few things you really need to pay extra special attention to for your rocket to fly properly:

- ✔ Make sure you securely attach the engine mount and engine hook. If this part of the rocket is weak, the rocket may fail right on the launch pad!

✔ Don't skimp on the fins. They, too, have to be securely attached to the rocket body. The rocket undergoes a lot of force at launch. You don't want the fins to fly off from the stress.

✔ The shock cord is the elastic string that attaches the parachute to the rocket body. Make it as long—or longer—than the plans call for. If it's too short, it might pull right out of the rocket at ejection.

Finish and paint your rocket however you like.

Adjust Your Rocket Kit

Depending on what size solar array you choose for your robot, you may have to choose a certain rocket to lift it into the air, or you can modify the kit to accommodate your rover. If you're not an old hand at building model rockets, I assume you won't try to modify the rocket. But here's the skinny: if you have a very large solar array, your rover's body may be too long to fit in a rocket like the V-2, but it will probably fit in a Pershing rocket body just fine (the Pershing is longer than the V-2).

If you want to put a long rover into a V-2 anyway, the modification is pretty simple. Model rockets with very fat bodies tend to use a tube-within-a-tube, like in this picture:

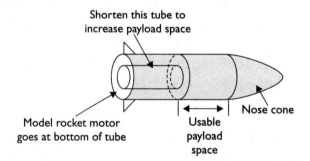

Shorten this tube to increase payload space

Nose cone

Model rocket motor goes at bottom of tube

Usable payload space

The narrow tube helps the ejection gases push the parachute and nose cone out at ejection time. But in the V-2, the smaller tube is so long that there's not enough room for a large rover inside. All you have to do is cut the narrow tube so it's about two inches shorter; then build it according to the plans. The end result will be that the tube won't extend as far into the top of the rocket, and you'll have more room to add a payload like the rover.

Building Little Sojourner

Our little solar-powered rover is pretty easy to make. In a lot of ways, it's little more than a solar array, a motor, and a few wheels thrown in for good measure. Little Sojourner has a problem, though: it has to fit in a model rocket body tube and survive "re-entry." What does that actually mean to us as we design and build it? It means two things:

✔ Little Sojourner can't be too large, or it won't fit in the rocket. Real roboticists have to deal with this problem all the time when they design bots for actual space missions—the robot has to fit on top of the rocket, and be light enough to be lofted all the way into space and to the planet it is trying to visit. It's a huge problem that takes a lot of the total time that goes into designing the space mission.

✔ Little Sojourner has to be built with some sort of recovery system. As you'll see, not only will it need to attach to a parachute, but it'll have to have some kind of release mechanism so the parachute can be left behind when the rover wants to drive away.

Now that we know what kind of problems we'll have to solve, let's build our robot:

I. The very heart and soul of the rover is the solar cell, so let's start with that (you can see the array I used, shown next). You can find solar arrays in many shapes and sizes at hobby shops and stores like Radio Shack. The array I chose for my Little Sojourner measures about $2\frac{1}{2} \times 3\frac{3}{4}$ inches. I found other solar arrays as small as $1\frac{7}{8} \times 3\frac{1}{8}$ inches that would work as well. Try fitting the solar array in your rocket body just to make sure it'll fit. Don't worry, we'll do a more scientific test later, but if the solar array won't fit in your rocket body all by itself, you need to get a bigger rocket or a smaller solar array. If all is well, put the rocket away and lay your solar array on a table.

 *Tip:* A lot of the measurements in this project are in sixteenths of an inch. Sixteenths are the smallest divisions you'll find on most rulers. Check out this ruler for a guide to common measurements on an ordinary ruler:

$\frac{1}{16}$ $\frac{5}{16}$ $\frac{11}{16}$

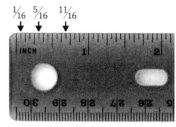

2. Now let's lay out all of the other major components around the array so we know how large to make the balsa robot body, as in the picture shown next. Notice that we're going to put the front wheel out in front of the solar array and the rear wheel behind the array. Why can't we just put the wheels under the solar array so the body isn't quite so long? That's a good question. We can't put the front wheel under the solar array since the wheel pops up through a slot in the body. Unless you want to cut a slot in the solar array (and then it wouldn't work anymore), you have to extend the body to put the motor and wheel up front. The rear wheels could go under the solar array if the axle is long enough, but it probably won't be—especially if you bought a standard set of Pinewood Derby racing wheels. Pinewood axles are $2\frac{1}{2}$ inches long, and there's just over $1\frac{3}{4}$ inches between the wheels when they're on the axle. That won't be long enough to stretch across most solar arrays. So we have to extend the balsa body behind the solar array and make it narrow enough for the Pinewood axle instead.

3. When all of your parts are laid out like in the picture, measure the length of the body from the front end of the front wheel all the way back to the axle holes of the rear wheels (for my solar array, it's about $5\frac{1}{4}$ inches).

4. When you know the total length and width of your rover body, use a hobby knife and a straight edge to cut the body out of $\frac{3}{32}$-inch balsa wood.

5. We need to trim the rover body down to a narrower width so the rear Pinewood wheels will fit. As we already said, the wheels will only be about $1\frac{3}{4}$ inches apart. Reduce the width of the body by cutting away about $\frac{11}{16}$ inches from each side of the body so it is only about $1\frac{5}{8}$ inches wide (or a little less). You can cut away the sides all the way to the front of the solar array, but don't go past the front end of the array—we'll work on the front later. You may want to make cut marks like this, so you don't accidentally cut the wrong parts away:

If you cut the body correctly, it should now look like this:

6. Slide the two wheels onto the axle and add the end caps that came in the package, trapping the wheels. Test fit the wheels on the back of the rover: hold the axle in place and make sure that the wheels can turn freely and aren't getting snagged on the side of the body.

7. Will the rover still fit in your rocket body? Now is a good time to test, before you build much more of the rover. Take the balsa body and insert it into the rocket tube. Can you put the nose cone on the body without running into the balsa body of the rover? Does it look like there's enough room to fit the wheels, too? Hold or tape the rear axle onto the body and make sure that the rover will still fit, even with the wheels on. If everything fits and you don't have to do any more trimming to get the wheels to turn, set the axle and wheels aside for a moment.

8. Now it's time to work on the front of the rover. Slide a wheel onto the end of the motor's spindle. If the spindle is larger than the wheel's hole, so it doesn't fit properly, use a drill to slightly enlarge the hole (this is almost certainly a step you'll need to grab an adult for). If the spindle is too small, and the wheel just flops around, wrap a little masking tape around the spindle until the wheel is simply snug. Don't use too much tape! Use just enough to hold the wheel on. Too much tape can get in the way and make the motor not work right. Also, make sure that the wheel is larger than the motor so that when you sit it on the ground, the wheel will touch, not the motor itself. If you need to, find a bigger wheel.

9. Next, we need to cut out the "wheel well," where the front wheel will rest. Begin by marking the center point, as shown:

10. Measure the wheel's width and diameter. Then mark these dimensions on the body, using the center mark from the previous step as a guide.

11. Carefully use a hobby knife to cut away the wheel well. Cut an extra 1/16 of an inch away on both sides of the wheel well, so it's a bit larger than the wheel itself. Then, hold the motor on the body and

check the fit—the wheel should have enough room in the wheel well so that it can turn freely.

12. Cut a square of balsa wood from some of the leftover balsa sheet that's about the same size as the motor. This will be the base that we can use to securely attach the motor to the robot. Be sure that the wood's "grain" will be perpendicular to the direction of the motor's spindle, as you can see in this picture:

13. Tear off about seven inches of masking tape and wrap the balsa and motor together. Wrap it very tightly, so there's no slack in the tape and you can't wiggle the balsa around inside the tape.

14. Showtime! Let's start attaching parts to the robot body. We'll begin with the rear wheels. Carefully remove the wheels from the axle. (Don't lose the end caps!) Mix some five-minute epoxy and use it to securely

cement the axle to the underside of the rear of the balsa body. Be sure that the axle is centered on the body and that there's enough space to reattach the wheels to the ends of the axle when you're done. Let it dry completely before you move on to the next step.

15. Decide which side of the body you plan to mount the motor on (it really doesn't matter), and cut the front side that won't have the motor flush with the back, as you can see next. Take the motor and, with some more epoxy, glue the balsa motor base to the underside of the body, making extra sure that the wheel sits right in the middle of the wheel well. Let the epoxy dry completely before you move on.

16. Add the rear wheels and axle caps again—the rover should now roll on a flat surface.

17. Now let's add the solar array. You could simply epoxy the bottom of the solar array to the top of the balsa body, but double-sided tape is a better solution. That makes it easy to move the array to a different body or change the solar array later if you want to modify your robot. Mark the position of the solar array on the top of the body so you know where to put the tape.

18. Stick the tape to the balsa body, cutting around the wheel well if you need to.

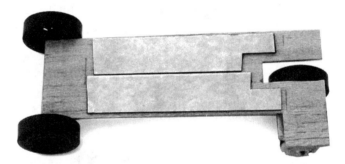

19. Pull the top layer off of the two-sided tape and carefully lay the array down on the body. Your robot should now look more or less like this:

You're about to find out how the rover will be carried to earth by parachute, yet be released when it reaches the ground. We're going to add a "parachute hook" to the rear of the rover. This hook hangs from the parachute during descent, but allows the parachute to drop off when it reaches the ground.

20. Take a length of brass rod and a pair of pliers. Bend it into shape, using these dimensions:

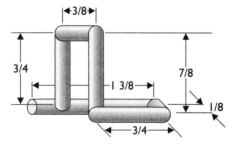

21. Now cut a new rectangle from the balsa sheet which will help hold the parachute hook in place on the rover body. It should measure about $1\frac{1}{2} \times \frac{3}{4}$ inches.

22. Using a drill bit, pin, or hobby knife, work a small hole into the balsa block through which the parachute hook can travel.

23. Push the parachute hook through the wood until the block is sitting right on top of the base of the hook.

24. Mix some more epoxy and put a generous amount on the top of the balsa body and the bottom of the block. Push the two together so the parachute hook is sandwiched between them, pointing out of the back of the robot. Hold it tightly for at least five minutes until the epoxy is dry and the parachute hook is secure.

25. Just one more step: attach the wires from the solar array to the wires coming out of the back of the motor. Temporarily attach the wires and test the circuit by holding Little Sojourner under a bright desk light or outdoors in the sunlight. Which way do the wheels turn? If the rover will roll backwards, swap the wires. If you have access to a soldering iron (and your folks can help), solder these connections permanently. If you can't solder, that's okay—just be sure to twist the wires securely. If there's a lot of loose wire hanging around, tape it to the bottom of the balsa body to get it out of the way.

That's Little Sojourner—if you take it outdoors, it should now roll on its own. Unless you line up the front and rear wheels absolutely perfectly, it should run in circles instead of a straight line. That's fine. Actually, you probably want it to make circles when it rolls; otherwise, it might run away after it parachutes to the ground and you'll never find it again. If it goes in circles, you know it will never stray too far from the landing point.

Making the Parachute

Most model rocket parachutes come almost fully assembled. Look for an 18-inch, pre-assembled parachute kit from Estes. If your Little Sojourner is a bit bigger than mine—if you used a bigger solar array, for instance—you might want to use a 24-inch parachute instead.

To complete the 'chute, all you need to do is connect it to a recovery cable. I used a Rhino Cable; you can get a bag of them for just a few dollars. Here is what they look like:

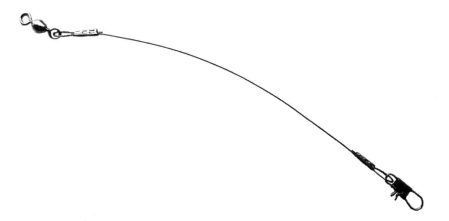

Unclip the "quick release" end of the cable and hook it through all the loops of the parachute (making sure not to tangle the parachute lines in the process). Clip the quick-release closed again, and test the parachute to make sure it's not tangled.

Testing the Recovery System

Would you get into an airplane no one ever tested? Ride in a car without seat belts? Get on a roller coaster no one ever rode before? Probably not—so don't put Little Sojourner in the rocket and blast it into the air without making sure the parachute recovery system will work properly first. Do this:

1. Take the other end of the recovery cable—the small end, without the quick release cable—and slide it onto the parachute hook on the back of the rover.

2. Hold the rover and parachute much like they'll be when they're packed in the rocket body. The rear wheels will be packed downward, and the parachute will be folded over the solar array.

3. Go to a somewhat high location—a second-story balcony or open window is perfect. Let go of the rover and parachute together.

If the rover works properly, the parachute will unfurl quickly, slowing the rover's descent. When the rover hits the ground, it's balanced to strike the bottom of the front wheel and, as long as it's not a very windy day, should settle down right side up on its three wheels. The parachute will fall to the ground, and the recovery cable will slip down the back of the parachute hook.

That's what is *supposed* to happen. Will it always work that way? Of course not! But you should test it a bunch of times and be confident that it works properly perhaps seven out of ten times before actually launching it. If you're having trouble getting the rover to come to the ground properly, grab someone to help you and try to figure out what you can do to make it more reliable.

Testing for Stability

If you're already a model rocket whiz and want to build your own Little Pathfinder from scratch to accommodate Little Sojourner, go right ahead! But be sure to test it for stability before you fly it. Even if you build your rocket from a kit, you might want to test your rocket, since the rover will change the basic design and weighting of the rocket slightly.

The basic idea behind rocket stability is this: you want the nose to always be in the front, and the tail to be in the back. Many early rocket tests didn't quite work: you may have seen old movies of NASA rockets flying end-over-end into the air, only to explode moments later.

So how do you know if your rocket is stable? Start by prepping the rocket for flight. Load it with a motor, wadding, parachutes, and insert the Little Sojourner rover. Then, get a long string (at least a few feet long) and tie one end of it around your rocket body so that you can hold the string and the rocket hangs in the air. Slide the string up and down the rocket body until the rocket is perfectly balanced—it hangs level with the ground. That is what we call the rocket's *center of mass*.

Now start to swing the rocket around you, as if you were holding a rope and planning to lasso a cow. Spin the rocket fast around you, over your head. The nose should stay pointed forward as it spins.

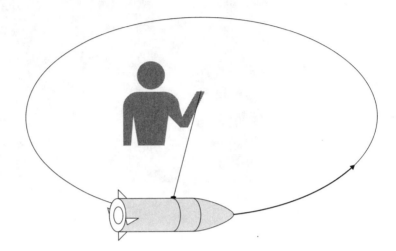

If it does, the rocket's *center of pressure* is behind the center of mass, and you're safe to launch. If the rocket spins around so the nose doesn't stay pointed forward, you have a problem—the center of pressure is in front of the center of mass, and your rocket won't fly. You can solve the problem easily by adding some weight to the front of the rocket. You can pack a little modeling clay in the nose cone, for instance, and then try the stability test again.

Launch Day

If you're already into model rocketry, great! You're ready to rock! If you don't know a lot about model rocketry, I suggest you visit the National Association of Rocketry's web site (it's at www.nar.org). NAR is an organization that can help you learn more about rocketry and how to launch rockets safely. You might also want to find a local rocket club and launch with them. The advantage of a rocket club is that they've already done the hard part of finding a good launch site, and they might even have a permit or agreement with the city to launch there.

When you pack Little Pathfinder for launch, be sure to use plenty of wadding to protect your payload. Carefully load Little Sojourner, front wheel facing up, with its parachute beside the bot, right on top of the solar array. Insert the rocket's parachute. Pack the rocket's parachutes beside the solar array as well, to prevent anything from getting tangled in the robot's wheels.

How Model Rockets Work

A model rocket is launched by electrically igniting an expendable solid-fuel motor. By expendable, I mean that the motor only works once—after that, you throw it away and use a new motor for the next launch. You insert an igniter in the engine, stand it on the launch pad, and then, after a short countdown, launch the rocket by pressing the ignition button which sends a small electrical charge to the rocket engine. The launch pad uses a long rod to keep the rocket pointed in the right direction for the first moment of launch; your rocket has a "launch lug," which looks like a soda straw, to guide the rocket along the rod.

Engines come in a variety of strengths. They're sold by letter (A, B, C, and so on) and the higher the letter, the more powerful the motor—so a C engine is more powerful than an A. Motors also have numbers, as in C6-3. The first number gives you a better idea of how much thrust you'll get from the rocket, and the final number tells you how long a delay there is, in seconds, between the end of the thrust phase of the rocket and when the parachute is ejected. The rocket only fires for a very short time; after that, it "coasts" higher and higher on the energy the engine initially delivered. After a few seconds of coast, another charge in the motor fires up, into the rocket body. Since this charge is very hot, you use a handful of non-flammable stuff called "wadding" to keep the parachute from catching on fire. When the ejection charge fires, though, it pushes the parachute out and the nose cone off the front of the rocket. After the parachute opens, it settles slowly back down to earth.

If all goes well during the launch (see Figure 4-3), and the landing site is smooth, you should catch up to a solar-powered rover exploring around the landing site.

Figure 4-3
With Little Sojourner safely tucked inside, Little Pathfinder (actually, an Estes V-2 kit) sits on the pad, ready for launch.

Here are some things that might go wrong:

Problem	Solution
If it's very windy, the parachute may not come off the parachute hook and end up dragging the poor little rover across the ground	Try to test Little Sojourner and launch Little Pathfinder when it's calm.
The parachute might fall down the wrong side of the parachute hook and not disengage	This shouldn't happen very often, but if it does, make sure the parachute hook is bent toward the rear, as you can see in the photos of the rover elsewhere in this project.
The parachute might disconnect from the rover at ejection, causing Little Sojourner to come plummeting to the ground	One time in a hundred this might happen. To minimize the chances of this happening, be absolutely sure the cable is pushed through the parachute hook when you load it into the rocket.
Little Sojourner doesn't move after it lands	The solar-powered motor doesn't have the juice to push it through grass. Try to recover the rocket on flat pavement, dirt, or tiny gravel—any surface that won't stop the wheels from turning

Improving Little Pathfinder

This is possibly the most complex project in the book, so don't be surprised if it takes a lot of trial and error to get it to work. As you work on the robot, you might consider some variations to make it a better or more interesting project:

✔ Can you come up with a more reliable parachute release system for Little Sojourner?

✔ What can you do to get Little Sojourner to travel through grass? Would adding a battery pack instead of the solar array help? Can you do that and still make it fit in Little Pathfinder?

✔ Try different solar arrays. Can you get better performance with different sets of solar cells?

✔ Can you modify Little Sojourner so you can adjust the size of the circle it makes when it runs on the ground?

PROJECT 5

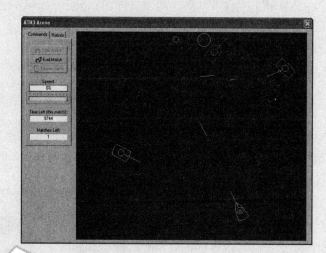

Combat on the Computer Screen

What You'll Need

✔ AT-Robots 3. Download a copy from the author at
www.nw.fmph.uniba.sk/~9bartelt
or from my own web site at
www.bydavejohnson.com

No matter where you download it, the program is free and requires Microsoft Windows 95, 98, ME, or XP. The program is actually very small and requires less than a megabyte of hard disk space, so it should run on almost any computer.

Time Required

About 10 hours

Difficulty

Advanced. It helps to know a little about computer programming or to have someone help you—especially if you want to make your own robots by modifying the robots I've provided for you in this project.

Project

Design and program four "virtual" combat robots that live only on the computer screen, then send them into combat using a free program called AT-Robots 3 (which you can see in Figure 5-1). Use the robots to experiment on your own, or compete against other people.

Figure 5-1
In this project, you'll create some combat robots and let them fight in a virtual world using your computer.

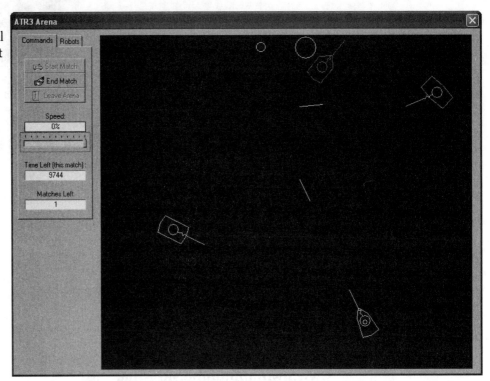

Introduction

Robots are all around us, but we don't always notice them. Why? Because many robots are not mechanical at all—they're computer programs designed to automate tasks that have to be done over and over and over. The ATM machine that spits out cash is a kind of robot. So is the search engine you use when looking for web pages on the Internet.

Once you realize that robots don't have to have mechanical bodies, it's easy to see that you can "build" robots that live entirely within a computer. That means you can experiment with very sophisticated, advanced robot concepts, since you can concentrate on making their "brains" work without worrying about building the actual robot body. People have taken that idea and made games in which you pit virtual robots against each other. Many of these games are played in colleges, where engineering students design fiendishly complicated bots that are really advancing the state of robotic science in a fun way. For the rest of us, we can try our hand at virtual robot combat using a program like AT-Robots 3. If you don't know much about computer programming, this project may look a bit scary. But don't worry—programming is not that hard, once you learn what the commands mean and the "syntax" of the language. Syntax is like grammar in English. Syntax is the correct order of words, numbers, and commands so the computer knows what you're trying to say. You wouldn't say,

Dog I walk the.

because no one would know you were trying to say, "I walk the dog." It's the same way with computers. You need to place commands in the right order, so

```
mov    5    <cookies>
```

means that you're storing the number 5 in a variable called "cookies." After that, you can use "cookies" anytime you need the number 5. But the parts of the command must all be in the right order for the computer to know what to do.

The Robots

Unlike our other projects, this is a robot you can make sitting at your computer. In fact, we're going to build four robots, each of which will show off special programming tricks that you can copy and use in your own robot designs. Here's what we're going to cook up:

✔ **Battle Station** The Battle Station is a stationary robot. No matter where it starts in the battle arena, it moves to a remote corner of the screen and stops there, where it fires a deadly barrage of laser pulses pretty much all the time (it doesn't use any kind of sensor to see if other robots are around).

✔ **Seeker** Seeker is not a very smart robot, but sometimes it gets lucky. This guy moves around the screen randomly, firing whenever its sensor tells it that there's another robot nearby.

✔ **Marauder** A deadly adversary, Marauder flies in circles, firing its guns at whatever might lay inside.

✔ **Interceptor** Interceptor has the potential to do the most damage of any robot, since it uses its sensors to lock onto enemy robots and follow them, firing from behind all the way.

These robots will be able to fight in a virtual combat arena. It'll look something like this:

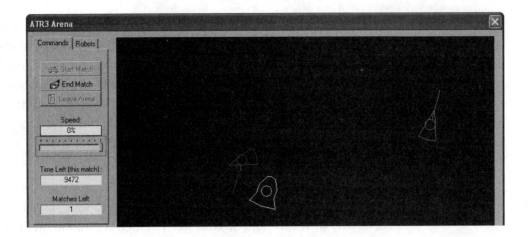

The Plan

This time out, our plan is quite simple. Since the robots are entirely "virtual," you'll create the robots in the AT-Robots 3 robot editor, then save and test them. To begin with, I'll teach you the basics of programming AT-Robots so you can have fun modifying existing bots and creating your own. After we cover the basics, I'll give you the program code to type into your PC to make Marauder. Since neither of us likes to do a lot of typing, though, here's a secret: all of the robots in this chapter are on my web site. Just type this web address into your computer's web browser:

www.bydavejohnson.com

Once you're there, follow the link to this book and you can download all the robots and load them right into AT-Robots without doing any more typing. And since all the robots come with tons and tons of comments explaining how they work, you can figure out what makes them tick and make your own special changes to them.

How to Download the Robots

If you're using Microsoft Internet Explorer, when you click on the robots at the web site, you'll see a dialog box pop up on the computer screen that asks whether you want to open the file or save it to your hard disk, like this:

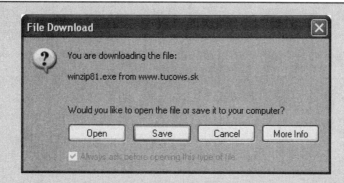

Choose to save it, and select a folder on your computer to store it in. You'll probably want to choose the same folder where you're keeping all your other robots.

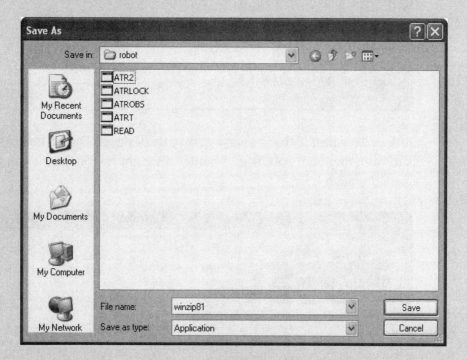

If you save the robots somewhere else, though, you can always "drag" the robots to a different folder later.

AT-Robots Basics

The AT-Robots 3 program is where you design, and test, your robots, then send them into combat on the computer screen. Start the program (double-click on the icon that says **ATR3,** as in the picture).

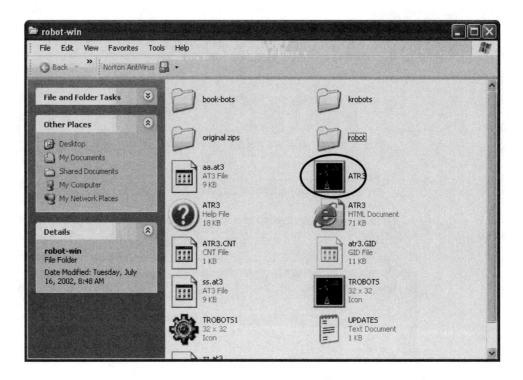

You'll see the AT-Robots window on your desktop. The left half of the window is for entering your robots into battle; the right half is where you design and change your robots.

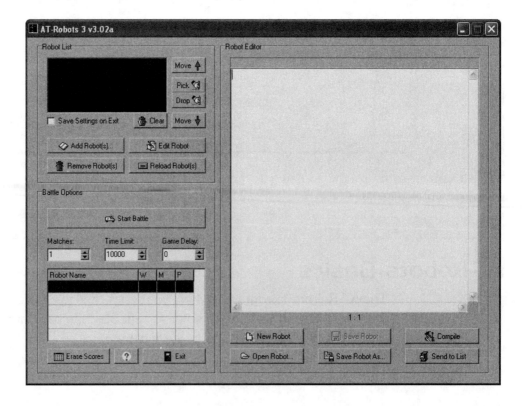

To design a robot, you type the program into the Robot Editor on the right side of the screen. The commands that you work with are very similar to a style of programming known as *assembly language*. And yeah, unlike Lego MindStorms programming, we have to type all of our commands into these robots—there are no little blocks to drag and drop. Your fingers will get a workout, but I think it'll all be worth it when you *see* your robots running around the screen, shooting at other robots.

Every robot program has the same basic format:

1. We start by defining the robot's design. We can name the robot, choose a color, and add parts. Your robot has a certain kind of hull, a weapon, scanners that can be used to look for other robots, and more. All of this goes in the beginning of the program.

2. We define our variables. Back in MindStorms, we often created variables to do things like keep score and count. We'll make variables to store numbers for our robots in this project as well, but we have to define all of them so the computer knows what to expect. We list them right after we design the robot's body.

3. Finally, we add the programming that tells the robot what to do.

There are a few other things you'll notice as we start to create our robot program:

✔ We use the **#** symbol at the start of some lines. These are "tags," and they are important because they tell the program that a new part of the program is starting. You'll use a tag to name the robot, give it a color, define the equipment that's on your robot, and start the programming itself.

✔ We use the **//** symbol (that's just two slashes, found under the **?** on the keyboard) to leave ourselves comments in the program. Comments remind us what the program is doing, so you can look at it again in a few weeks and remember what the program means. You can write anything after a **//** symbol, and the program ignores it. Those comments are just for you and whoever else reads your program.

Check out Figure 5-2. You can see tags and comment marks in this robot.

Figure 5-2
Right now, it all looks like gobbledygook. But in a few pages, you'll know exactly what this stuff means!

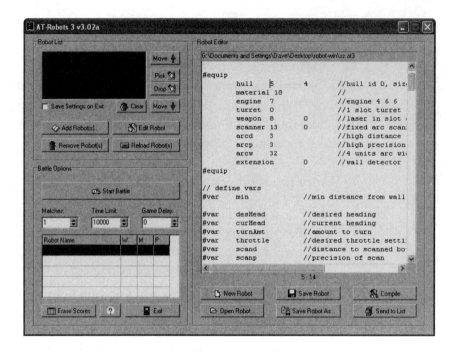

Make a Simple Test Robot

Ready to start? Let's create a simple robot. Do this:

1. Open the program and make sure that the Robot Editor on the right side of the screen is empty. If there's anything in it, click the New Robot button at the bottom of the screen.

2. Type the following lines into the editor. You don't have to include the comments unless you want to:

```
#name testy        //we named the robot testy
#color $ff0000     //the robot will be colored blue
```

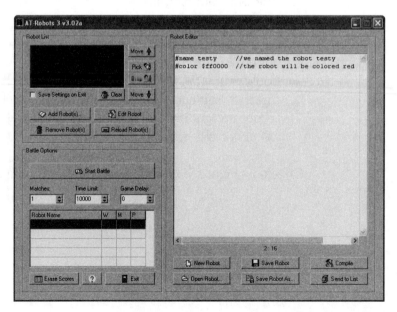

You can color your bot anything you like, but you need to use the *hexadecimal* (a number system based on 16 instead of 10) color equivalents for blue, green, and red. Zero means no color at all, while the highest value (which is the letter f) means the maximum color.

Here are a few sample colors you can use, but you can also experiment by "mixing" red, green, and blue to make your own robot colors:

Hexadecimal Code	Color
ff0000	Blue
00ff00	Green
0000ff	Red
ffffff	White
000000	Black (not good unless you want your bot to be invisible against the black background)
00ffff	Yellow
ff00ff	Purple

The next tag in the program is #equip. This lists all of the equipment that the robot is armed with—like the hull size and material, engines, weapons, and scanners. You can find lists of all the equipment in the AT-Robots user guide. There are 20 different hulls, for instance, and each one has a different shape. Hulls also come in four sizes, from smallest to largest. Bigger hulls can carry more stuff. After we assign a hull, we need to tell the program what it is made from. You can choose from a wide variety of building materials, like tin, silver, iron, gold, and iridium. Which material should you pick? That's a good question—the heavier the material, the more battle damage it can take, but it's also heavier, which means you can't carry as many weapons.

3. Let's continue building our Testy bot by throwing in a few materials:

```
#equip
      hull      0   4   //hull 0 is a triangle, and size 4 is the
largest body
      material    5   //material 5 is lead
#equip                 //remember to start and end the equipment
section with an equip tag
```

Anxious to see what this robot looks like? Just a few more steps:

4. Add one more line to this bot:

```
#begin   //after this comes the robot's actual program instructions
```

5. Save the robot by clicking Save Robot As... and give it a name. It should look like this:

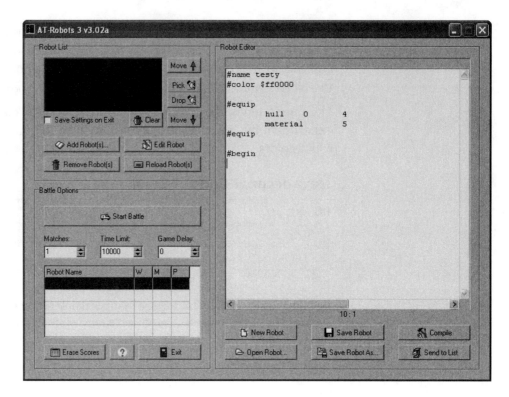

6. Let's make sure that the robot isn't over its weight limit. Remember, each hull can only carry so much weight. Click the Compile button. It doesn't really compile anything—that's programmer talk for "getting the program ready to run." What this button really does is tell you what the robot actually weighs. You should see that we're way under the weight limit, so we're ready to move on. If the robot had weighed too much, we'd have to make the hull bigger, the material lighter, or remove some equipment.

7. Click OK to close the Information box that tells us what the robot weighs.

8. Now, on the left side of the window, click Add Robot(s)... and load Testy as well as one other sample robot. If Testy is the only robot you have, just load it twice.

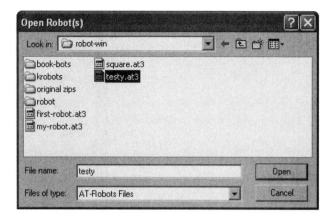

9. Check both boxes in the Robot List. This tells the program to add them to the battle.

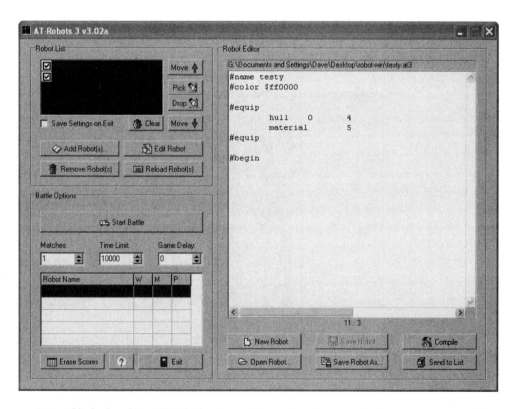

10. Click the Start Battle button. When the Arena window opens, you'll see some buttons on the left side of the screen. These let you start and stop the battle.

II. Click the Start Match button to see your Testy onscreen. See? Isn't it cute?

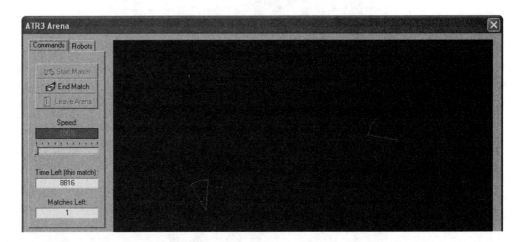

When you're satisfied, click End Match and then click Leave Arena to get back to where we started.

Make the Robot Move and Shoot

That's a simple robot that can't even move; it just sits around looking blue and triangular. If you want to make it move, you'll need to add an engine. That's easy, since it goes in the **#equip** section; simply pick one from the list in the user guide. You have a lot of choices listed in the AT-Robots user manual; some are faster, some are slower, and the better engines weigh more (using up your valuable payload space). In fact, let's add an engine and a weapon at the same time. Modify your **#equip** section so it looks like this:

```
#equip
        hull        0    4
        material    5
        engine      7
        turret      1          //2 slot turret, slots at 0 and 128
        weapon      8    0     //laser in slot at 0
        weapon      8    128   //another laser in slot at angle 128
#equip
```

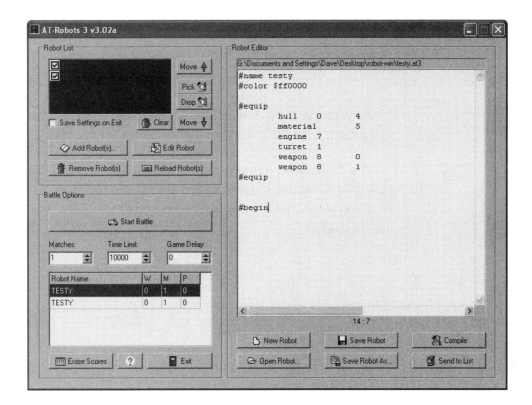

We added a mid-sized engine and a turret to this robot. No matter what kind of weapon you want to put on your robot, it must be mounted on a turret. (Imagine a tank—the big gun goes on a turret. It can't just hang in the air.)

There are five turrets available, and each one has a different number of slots in which you can put your weapons. I chose a two-slotted turret, and put a laser (that's weapon number 8) in each slot.

If you know how to read a compass, you might find the turret kind of funny. Instead of 360 degrees like an ordinary compass, AT-Robots uses a 256-degree compass. East is 0 and west is 128, as in the picture:

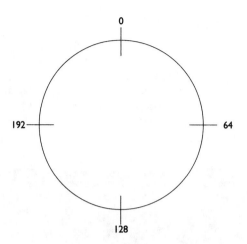

So whenever you deal with directions in AT-Robots, you need to remember to go from 0 to 255, not from 1 to 360.

You're probably getting anxious to see this robot in action. If you tried it out now, you'd find that it would still just sit there—we haven't programmed it to do anything yet. So let's add a few commands that will tell the robot to move and fire its lasers:

```
#begin
        out     10    5      //set throttle to 5%
@fire   out     41    0
        out     40    0
        out     41    1
        out     40    1
        jmp     @fire
```

So what does all this stuff do? First, let's watch it in action, then I'll explain it.

I.   After entering all the new commands, click the Save Robot button.

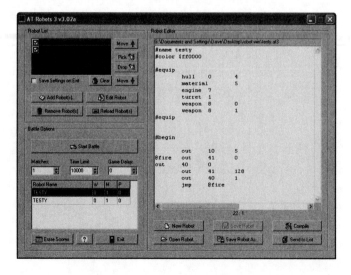

2. Since we just added equipment to the robot, let's check to see that the robot isn't too heavy. Click the Compile button. We're still way under the weight limit, so we're ready to move on.

3. Make sure that the robot is still selected in the Robot List (click on it in the list if you need to).

4. Click the Reload Robots button. You'll need to save, select, and reload every time you make a change to your robot to see it in the arena.

5. Finally, click Start Battle, then click Start Match once you're in the arena. Watch the fireworks!

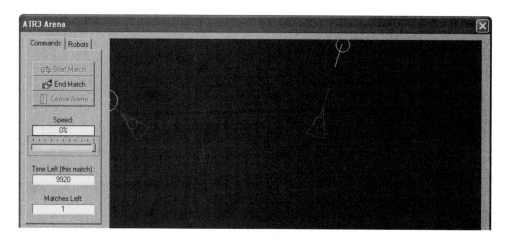

Ready to find out what happened? Well, the first thing you should know is that we use two important commands in AT-Robots: **in** and **out**, short for input and output. If you want to find out something, like the temperature of the laser gun (it heats up as it fires), you'd use **in**. If you want to *do* something to your robot, like turn on the engine or fire the gun, you use **out**.

We also need to look at the user guide to see the list of all the input and output *ports*. There's a port for everything on the robot; when you want the robot to do something, you have to send a command to the correct port. It's like pushing a button to turn on your TV, except you can think of the TV's power switch as a port—and you just send the "on" command to that port.

To move very slowly by setting the engine to 5 percent throttle, for instance, you output the number 5 to port 10 (if you look it up, you'll find that 10 is the

engine). Want to select a weapon? That's port 41, followed by the slot in the turret it's mounted in. Time to fire a weapon? Output to port 40. So in the program, we're setting the throttle to 5 percent, then firing the weapons.

Since we want to fire the lasers over and over, it's easiest to use a subroutine (like the routines we wrote in Lego MindStorms). In AT-Robots, we always start a subroutine with a label that has the @ symbol, as in **@fire1**. After firing the weapons, we jump ("**jmp**") back to **@fire1** and do it all over again…

Well, until our robot explodes because the lasers overheated. The lasers are neat, and they never need to be reloaded with ammunition like some weapons, but we have to keep them cool by not firing them too much. Here's how we could fix the robot to keep it from blowing up:

```
#var    heat
#begin
        out    10      5         //set the robot's speed
@fire1  out    41      0         //select the first laser
        in     48      <heat>    //find out the laser's temperature
        cmp    <heat>  225       //compare current temp to 225
        jg     @fire2            //if it's greater, go to fire2
        out    40      0         //fire the laser
@fire2  out    41      1         //select the second laser
        in     48      <heat>
        cmp    <heat>  225
        jg     @fire1
        out    40      0
        jmp    @fire1
```

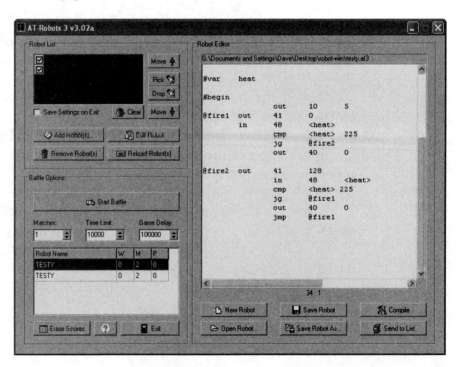

First, we added a variable—we have to define them right after the #equip section but before #begin. Once we create a variable called **heat**, we can tell Testy to keep an eye on the temperature of the laser; before it fires, it compares ("**cmp**") the temperature of the weapon to 225, which is almost dangerously hot according to the AT-Robots manual for lasers. If the variable called heat is 225 or more, it skips firing and tries the next laser (**jg** stands for "jump if greater than"). And since we have more than one weapon on the robot, we need to use port 41 to tell the robot which weapon to use. We set port 41 to either 0 or 1, depending on which turret slot we want to use.

Run the battle again and notice that the lasers fire really fast at first—until they heat up—and then the rate of fire slows down for the rest of the battle.

So far so good? Great! Now it's time to build some robots you can really fight with. You might want to keep Testy around for more experiments, but for now let's move on and make Marauder.

Building Marauder

By now, you probably know the drill. To create a new robot, click the New Robot button and start typing into the Robot Editor. If you don't want to type this whole program, you can download it in finished form directly from my web site—check the section, "Downloading the Robots," for info on how to do that. Remember that you can save yourself a lot of time by not typing in all the comments; they're just there to help you understand what the robot does.

As you can see next, this robot really only has half a dozen commands in the main part of the program. Try to follow the program through, as if it were a road map taking you across town. Here's what you should see:

✔ We create the robot by assigning a name, a color, and equipment. The bot has one weapon and a scanner to look for other bots.

✔ We create a bunch of variables that we'll need as the program runs.

✔ When the program begins, we first set how tightly Maurauder will turn by putting a number in **turnAmt**. You can easily change that number to see how it affects the bot's performance.

✔ Next, we set the speed of the engine with **throttle**. Again, you can change that number to see how well a faster or slower bot performs.

✔ The main subroutine is only six lines long, and that includes a line back to the beginning of the subroutine! First, we turn, then we scan for other bots. If a bot is found, we fire the laser. If not, we go back to the beginning again.

✔ The rest of the program is a bunch of subroutines that the main part of the program calls for. You should be able to figure it all out by reading the lines aloud and checking what the port numbers do in the program's user guide.

```
#name Marauder
#color $0000FF

#equip
    hull        0    4   // large, triangle shape
    material    19       // titanium
    engine      7        // average engine
    turret      0        // 1-slot-turret
    weapon      8    0   // the laser is at slot 0
    scanner     11   0   // D-F-Arc scanner on slot 0
    arcd        3    0   // range the scanner can see
    arcw        6    0   // width the scanner can see
#equip

#var turnAmt   //amount of each turn
#var random    //holds a random number
#var temp      //weapon temperature
#var found     //found another bot? if yes, found = 1
#var scan      //scanner scan value 1 (distance to nearest bot)
#var throttle

#begin
mov       <turnAmt>   5  // experiment; bigger numbers create a tighter turn
    mov   <throttle> 100 //experiment; this sets engine to max, but try slower
call      @setTurn
    call  @throttle

@main     call    @makeTurn
    call  @scan
    cmp   <found>     1   //was a bot found?
    jne   @main           //if not (jump not equal), then go to start
call      @fire           //otherwise, fire!!!
          jmp   @main      //jump to start

@throttle   out    10      <throttle> //run engine at number in "throttle"
ret

//setTurn decides which direction to turn at start of battle
//it gets a random number (max random number is 32767)
//if the random number is greater than max/2, turn right
//if less than max/2, the turnAmt is negated, so the bot turn left
@setTurn   in    0        <random>   // get random number
           cmp   <random> 16384      // compare to half-maximum
           jg    @nothing            // if greater, just return
           neg   <turnAmt>           // else, turn the other way
@nothing nop                         //nop stands for "no operation"
ret

//Subroutine makeTurn
//turns robot by amount in <turnAmt> variable
@makeTurn    out    11      <turnAmt> //turn the amount in the "turnAmt"
                                      //variable
```

```
                                            :
                                            :
      ret

      @fire    in      48   <temp>   //get the heat
         cmp   <temp>  225           //compare temp to 225
         jg    @nofire               //jump if greater to end and don't fire
         out   40      0             //fire weapon with 0 correction
      @nofire  nop
      ret

      //Subroutine scan
      //scans for a bot in the scanner
      //if a bot is found then distance is a positive number
      // (distance is -1 if a bot is not detected)
      @scan    mov    <found>   0
         in    50     <scan>    //check the scanner for a robot
         cmp   <scan>  -1
         je    @nobot            //then no bot on scanner, so return
         mov   <found>  1        //else set found flag
      @nobot   nop
      ret
```

Time for Battle

Once you've finished your Marauder, let's try to pit it against another Marauder just to see what a battle is like. When you make more robots, you can see what different programming tactics and different robot hulls, weapons, and engines can do. But for now, let's try this:

1. Save Marauder to your hard drive by clicking the Save Robot As button and giving it a name.

2. Next, change the hull shape to something else, like a square. Now we'll be able to tell them apart in battle.

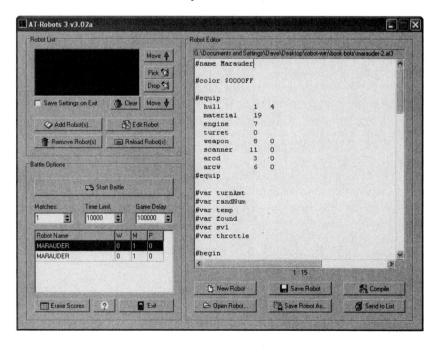

3. You might also want to change the robot's name in the top line of the program and perhaps even its color.

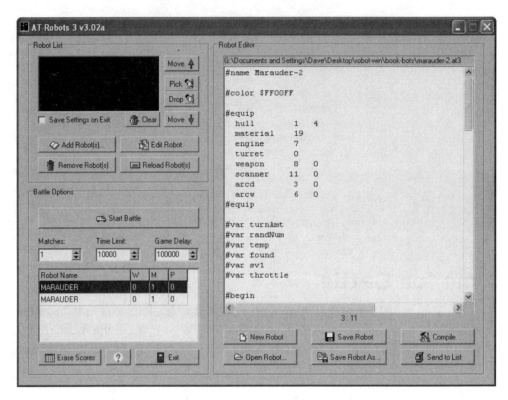

4. Save this version of Marauder with a different filename, again with the Save Robot As button.

5. Now it's time to add them to the Robot List. Click the Add Robots button and add them to the list.

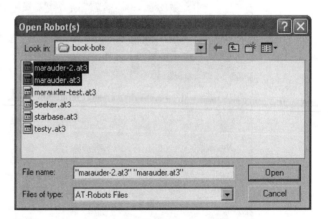

6. Check the boxes beside both robots in the list.

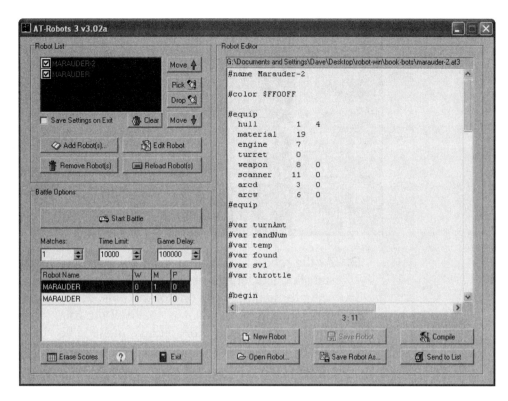

7. Click the Start Battle button and you'll be swept away to the arena. Look for the slider that controls the speed of the battle and slide it all the way to the left, so the battle runs slowly.

8. Finally, click the Start Match button to watch the excitement.

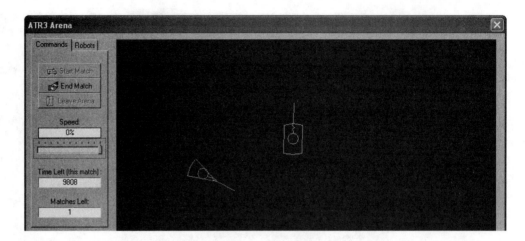

9. As the robots are fighting, you might want to take a look at their statistics, like which one is winning. Click the Robots tab and you'll see information about one of the bots. The big bar that looks like a fuel gauge is the remaining health of the robot. Click on the first robot name and you'll see a drop-down menu which you can use to select a different robot. Pick the other robot so you can see both robots onscreen at once.

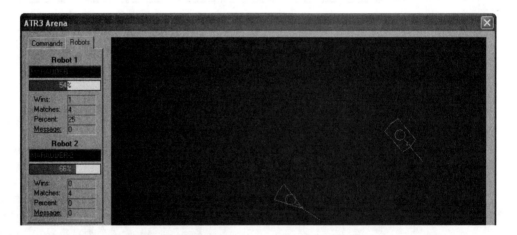

10. When the match is complete, click on the Commands tab and click the Leave button to return to the main screen.

You can follow those same steps to start battles and watch their progress, no matter how many robots you want to throw into the arena at once. Just remember: You can only look at the health of two robots at once, since there are only two stats boxes. So you'll just have to keep changing the view to a different robot if you're battling more than two at once.

Downloading the Robots

Once you have tried Marauder, you probably won't want to do much more typing. The rest of the robots in this project—Battle Station, Seeker, and Interceptor—are all waiting for you on my web site. Open the web browser on your computer and go to:

www.bydavejohnson.com

Find the robots and click on them. Choose to save them to your hard disk in the folder on your PC where you're keeping all of your other AT-Robots. After you've done that, you should be able to load them into the program and make them battle each other.

Another Virtual Robot

AT-Robots 3 is a lot of fun once you figure out its confusing language. And there's a real challenge in getting your bot to behave the way you think it should. Just the thing for a rainy Saturday afternoon! If you want another computer robot challenge that is a little easier to master, look into a program called MindRover. You can download it from **www.mindrover.com**. There's a free demo that lets you try out a few robots and get a feel for how it all works. If you like it, you can buy the game for about $25. For another $15, you can even get the MindRover RCX Pack Add-On, which lets you program Lego MindStorms robots with MindRover.

Unlike AT-Robots, you do all your programming by dragging and dropping stuff. To create a robot, for instance, just drag the right parts—like sensors, motors, and weapons—onto the robot body.

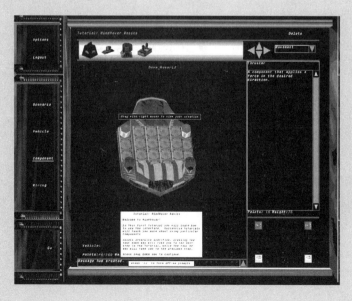

To program the robot, you create "circuits" by dragging connections between the various parts of the robot. To turn, for instance, wire the thruster directly to the sensor, so it'll run whenever it sees an enemy robot.

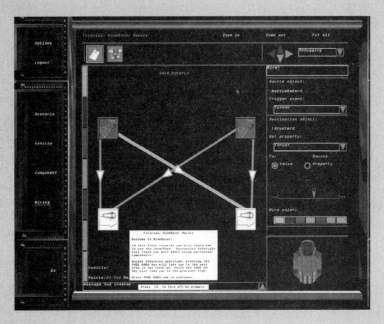

Other tasks require you to use *logic circuits*—you might only fire the rockets if you can see the enemy with both sensors, for instance. That would use an **AND** circuit.

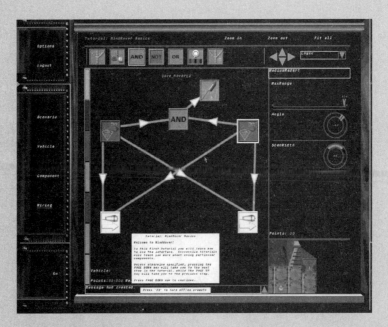

When you're done programming your robot, you can turn it loose in a 3D environment that looks like your living room.

Improving Your AT-Robots

Once you understand the basics of programming your robot in AT-Robots 3, the sky is the limit. Here are a few things you might try programming. See how efficient you can make your robot. And check my web site—you may sometimes find some new robots to try out!

✔ When you hit the wall, you take damage. Even the collision avoidance routine in Seeker and Interceptor doesn't work 100 percent of the time. Can you make it more efficient?

✔ Add other weapons to your turrets and try firing weapons that you have to reload.

✔ Can you program a robot like Seeker to change the angle it's firing at slightly as it tries hitting the target? Sometimes it'll try to lock onto a robot but be off slightly and not hit it. But if the weapon wobbled back and forth as it fired, you'd stand a better chance of striking the target.

✔ Program a robot to identify and not fire on allies. That way, you can have a "team" play in which robots can play two-on-two.

PROJECT 6

Remote-Controlled VideoBot

What You'll Need

- ✔ A remote controlled car
- ✔ A digital camera that has a video-out connection for a television
- ✔ A small tabletop tripod
- ✔ Wooden blocks, cardboard boxes, or other stuff to build a maze
- ✔ A tripod, coat rack, or some other tall stand
- ✔ Epoxy
- ✔ Heavy-duty, wide mailing tape
- ✔ Either:
    - ✔ X-10 or Radio Shack wireless transmitter and a long extension cord *or*
    - ✔ A long composite video cable (about 20 feet) and a male-to-male RCA cable connector

Time Required

About 2 hours

Difficulty

Simple. Once you get the parts, you should be able to assemble this quickly and do a lot of experimenting on your own.

6

Project

Modify an inexpensive remote-controlled car and a digital camera to act like a remote-controlled robot. The robot will transmit video to a television so you can steer the bot through a maze just by watching the on-robot video.

Introduction

The ideal robot is one that can handle complex tasks all on its own—like a deep-space robot that is so far from earth, it can't wait for instructions. Instead, the bot evaluates its situation and then acts all by itself.

Not all robots are autonomous, though. Many robots are remote-controlled by humans who steer them, operate their arms, claws, or grabbers, and make all the important decisions. Some robots like this are the combat robots you see on television. Others are used by police, firefighters, and bomb squads to go places too dangerous for people. Some robots operate underwater—they're fancy submarines driven by marine scientists who wait on the surface with elaborate remote controls.

In this project, we'll make a robot like that—a robot you get to control from a remote control. Not only will this show you what it's like to be a human robot operator, driving a research robot into the heart of a volcano, but it also shows you something else. It shows you what a robot sees. If you grow up to design robots, you'll probably equip your bot with a camera so it can find its way around. And, it'll have vision that's a lot like the robot we're about to build. So get used to the view, because you may someday teach a robot how to move around by interpreting this kind of vision.

The Robot

Figure 6-1 shows a picture of Cyclops, our one-eyed robot. Cyclops is a very simple robot to build, since it's based on any old radio-controlled car you already have lying around the house. If you don't already have one, you can get an R/C car from Radio Shack for as little as $20. How do we get the video from the digital camera to a television, you're probably wondering. There are two ways, and you can try either one (or both, if you want to):

✔ Use a very long video cable to connect the camera directly to the television. Downside: The robot must be run in the same room as the TV.

✔ Attach the camera to a wireless video transmitter. The great thing about this approach is that you can set up your maze in any room

Figure 6-1
Cyclops is an R/C car that we've equipped with a digital camera for vision and a transmitter to send the video to a television—so you can pilot it remotely.

in the house. Downside: Since I couldn't find a transmitter that ran on batteries, you'll still need to connect a wire to the robot. The only difference is that this time, the wire is a power cable that plugs the transmitter into the wall.

The Plan

We'll start by creating Cylcops, our videobot. I'll show you how to make both versions—the wireless and the wired one. Then, we'll set up a maze and challenge you to drive through it only using the video on the television. You can't peek at the real maze and the robot's position in it. This is a lot like the way robot drivers have to steer their bots, since all they can see is what's on the video camera mounted in the robot.

Building Cyclops

We really only need three things to build Cyclops—the rest, which we'll get to later, is just the "ground support." We need three things:

✔ A tabletop tripod
✔ An R/C car
✔ A digital camera with a video output

A tripod is a three-legged support that photographers use to hold up a camera. You can pick one up in almost any camera shop. Most tripods are big, long-legged things that stand as high as a person. You can find tabletop tripods, however, that have legs just a few inches long. Look for the smallest tripod you can find.

Mine has legs that are four inches each. There's really no such thing as a tripod that's too small for this project, but make sure it has a normal screw mount on top where the camera can be attached.

As for the R/C car, get one that you don't mind turning into a robot. I used an Aggressor R/C car from Radio Shack, which cost about $25 (you can see it before the modification in Figure 6-2), but it really, really doesn't matter what kind of car you choose. The smaller your robot is, the smaller your maze can be, and that's something to consider if you have a small room to experiment with. Large cars turn into large robots with bigger turning circles.

Figure 6-2
The Aggressor is an inexpensive R/C car that I chose to turn into Cyclops.

Finally, you need a digital camera. Let's talk about that a bit.

Test the Camera

In order to complete this project, you'll need to borrow your family's digital camera. Any camera will do; I used a Toshiba camera, shown in Figure 6-3. The camera needs to have a tripod mount on the bottom to screw into the tabletop tripod. It also needs a "video-out" connection, which lets the camera attach to a television or VCR.

Figure 6-3
A compact digital camera works best, since larger cameras might be hard to mount on the robot.

This video feature is included in most digital cameras; you usually just plug the special cable that comes in the camera box into the camera and then attach the other end to the video-in on a TV or VCR.

It is there so you can show pictures from the camera on a TV, like a video slideshow, but we're going to use it in a different way. We're going to use the video connection to broadcast live video from the camera on the TV.

Before we attach it to the car, though, let's make sure that it'll work the way we need. Attach the camera to a television using the video cable that came with the camera. Usually, you'd now set the camera to its "playback" mode and look at images stored on the memory card. Don't do that. Set the cameras to camera mode—so it's ready to take pictures—and turn the camera on. Turn on the TV,

and you should see whatever the camera sees. Wave the camera around, and you'll see the room on the television.

Not working? Try these fixes:

✔ Is the camera ready to take pictures? If it's on the wrong mode, you won't see anything on the TV.

✔ Is the TV set to the right input? You need to tell the TV or VCR where to look for the camera's video signal. It's probably labeled something like "External 1." If you need to, get someone's help to configure the TV.

✔ Are the batteries fresh? If the batteries in the camera are almost dead, it may not send the video signal out through the video cable.

✔ Is there a memory card in the camera? Some cameras won't work at all if the memory card slot is empty.

Once you see the video on the TV, you know that the camera works and you can turn it off for now. If you can't get the video to appear on your TV no matter what you try, you'll have to borrow someone else's digital camera to complete this project.

Put the Parts Together

You can make Cyclops as temporary or permanent as you like. I suggest, for instance, using epoxy to glue the tripod onto the hood of your car. If you want to use the car as a nonrobot again sometime in the future, though, you might not want to make the connection quite that permanent. Instead, you might want to use heavy-duty mailing tape.

Before you start missing epoxy or peeling tape, though, attach the camera to the tripod by firmly screwing them together.

Next, decide where the camera is going to go on your robot. Unfold the legs of the tripod and experiment with different locations on the front and top of the car. You should be able to find a spot in which the camera sits close to the ground, close to the car body. Check out the arrangement I've chosen for my Cyclops:

Once you know where the camera and tripod should go, use tape or epoxy to secure the tripod to the car body. Don't glue the camera to the tripod! You'll want to be able to remove the camera so mom can take pictures later—she won't appreciate having to hold the entire robot up to her eyes to take pictures in the future.

Wiring the Camera

The next step is to configure the camera so it plays on a television while we're actually operating the robot. As you probably read earlier in the chapter, there are two ways to do this, depending on where you plan to set up your robot maze and how complex you want the project to become. You can wire the robot directly to the television or use a wireless transmitter—decide which version of Cyclops you want to build, and then follow the instructions in this project.

Make a Direct Connection

If you want to connect Cyclops directly to a television, you'll need to set up the robot in the same room as the TV. Get a long length of composite video cable—it is the kind with an RCA connector at each end, like the one in the picture.

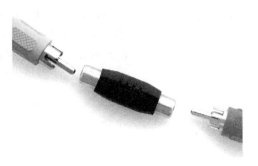

About 20 feet should be enough, though you may want your video cable to be even longer, depending on the size of the room. You don't have to buy a single, really long cable. You can connect several small lengths of video cable together to make one long cable—that's really handy if you already own a few short video cables. To do that, you'll need a video cable coupler from any electronics store. It looks like this:

You simply plug two video cables into this little gadget to turn the two cables into a long one.

You'll also need a coupler to connect the camera's cable to the long video cable. When you are sure you have enough parts, follow these steps:

1. Plug the digital camera's video cable into the camera.
2. Attach a video coupler and attach the long video cable to the coupler.

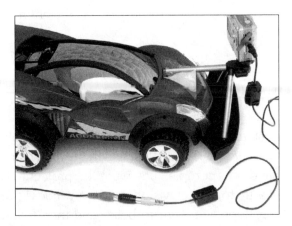

3. If you need to, add additional couplers and extend the length of the cable with extra, shorter cables.
4. Plug the other end of the video cable into your TV or VCR.

5. Make sure the TV is set for the right input so the robot's video will appear onscreen.

That's all there is to it. Your robot is now ready for action; skip ahead to the section called "Making the Maze" to finish the project.

Make a Wireless Connection

The wireless approach is great if you have a large, open room to create your maze, but the family TV is in another room. You could even set the maze up outdoors and really go wild with a huge maze, as long as you have access to an outdoor electrical outlet.

In order to build this version of Cyclops, you need to have a wireless video transmitter. There are two inexpensive models for sale (and, in fact, they're really the same gadget sold by two different companies). You can get the transmitter from either:

✔ X10.com. This is a web site that sells all sorts of home automation and wireless gadgets.

✔ Radio Shack

Both transmitters look a lot like this:

To turn Cyclops into a wireless robot, do this:

1. Identify the transmitter and receiver. You can tell which module is which because the transmitter, which will sit on the robot, has a bunch of connectors marked **IN**, while the receiver, which connects to the TV, has connectors marked **OUT** (see Figure 6-4). They might also be marked—the transmitter might be labeled **Transmitter** or **Sender**, for instance, while the receiver will probably just say **Receiver**.

2. Connect the receiver to your TV or VCR. To do that, take a short composite video cable and plug one end into the **Video-IN** port of

Figure 6-4
The Video-OUT connector on the receiver goes to the television, while the Video-IN connector on the transmitter receives video from the digital camera.

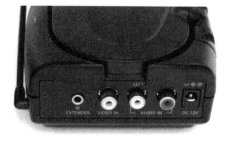

your TV or VCR. Then, plug the other end into the **Video-OUT** port of the receiver.

3. Plug the receiver into a wall outlet and turn it on.

4. Next, we need to make sure the transmitter and receiver can communicate with each other before we get too far along building the robot. We'll temporarily attach the transmitter to the digital camera. Take the video cable that came with the camera and plug one end into the camera and plug the other end into the **Video-IN** port on the transmitter.

5. Now, plug the transmitter into the wall outlet and turn on the transmitter by pressing the power switch.

6. Turn on your television and make sure it's set to the right video source so it sees the receiver on the **Video-IN** port.

7. Turn on the digital camera. You should see the camera's video on the television. If you don't, you may need to change the channel that the transmitter is broadcasting with. Turn the transmitter and receiver

upside down so you can see the channel slider, as in the next image. Make sure they're both set to the same channel: **A**, **B**, **C**, or **D**. If the video is distorted or there's a lot of interference, try changing the channel. When you've set both the transmitter and receiver to a channel setting that gives you good results, turn off both units and turn off the digital camera, too.

8. Now it's time to attach the wireless transmitter to the robot. Just like with the digital camera tripod, you can permanently connect it with some epoxy, or use some wide, heavy-duty tape to temporarily attach it to the robot.

9. If it's not still connected from step 4, take the video cable that came with the camera and plug one end into the camera and plug the other end into the **Video-IN** port on the transmitter.

10. Make sure that the AC adapter is still plugged into the power port on the transmitter. Then, take a short length of tape and secure the AC adapter itself to the robot. Why? Because the AC adapter is big and heavy, and we don't want it swinging around in the air when the robot is driving around. So we'll attach it to the robot and then only the extension cord is free in the air.

II. Plug a long extension cord (about 20 feet long, if possible) into the AC adapter that's now firmly attached to the robot. Plug the other end into the wall.

You're almost ready to roll (sorry about the pun). Turn everything back on and make sure that you can still see the digital camera's video on the television. If you can, you're ready to make a maze.

Making the Maze

This is the fun part: it's time to build a maze—like the kind you'd make a rat run through for some cheese—that Cyclops can drive through.

You can make the maze out of almost any building material (see Figure 6-5). Wooden blocks work great. You can also use cardboard boxes, plastic tubs, or anything else that you can arrange in a wall-like pattern. The goal of the maze should be to drive from a starting point just outside the maze to an exit point on the other side of the room.

Figure 6-5
This maze, made from wooden blocks, will test your ability to drive a robot when you can only see what's right in front of the bot, through its own eyes.

When you build your maze, make sure the walls are high enough to get into the digital camera's field of view. Remember: Cyclops' camera will be your eyes as you try to drive around the maze. That means that if your camera can peer over the walls of the maze, then you won't be able to drive the maze successfully!

Stringing the Cord

With all the other ingredients in place, the last piece of the puzzle is what to do with the long video cord or extension cord. Here's where the tripod or coatrack comes in handy. Stand it near the maze and attach the cord to the top of it, so the cord hangs high over the top of the maze. When you run Cyclops, use a helper—position someone near the cord stand to help keep the cord from falling down into the maze as the robot rolls around. You can take turns with the helper to alternate driving the robot and managing the cord.

Running the Maze

This should give you a good idea of what it's like to actually command a remote-controlled robot, like the kind emergency workers use to explore dangerous locations. You might be surprised at just how different the world looks through the eyes of a small robot that's sitting low to the ground and driving through your house. Here are some tips for getting Cyclops to run the way you want:

- ✔ When you run the bot, go easy on the throttle. The R/C car can probably run a lot faster than you can respond to obstacles, so only give it a little power when you move.

- ✔ Stop often. By stopping a lot, you can see where obstacles are and decide where and when to turn before you're already knocking down walls of blocks.

- ✔ Zoom out. If the camera comes with a zoom lens, zoom way out to the "widest" possible view. If you are zoomed in, everything will look closer than it really is and the camera may have trouble focusing (so everything will look blurry).

- ✔ If you find the camera turns off after just a minute or two, check the camera's settings. There's probably a control that tells the camera not to turn itself off, or to wait longer before shutting off to conserve battery power.

6

Improving Cyclops

It's pretty cool to use a remote control to drive a robot around, seeing only through the bot's own eyes. Once you get tired of the maze, though, there are some other things you might try to make this project even better:

✔ *Try robot combat.* With a wedge-shaped piece of wood or plastic, you can add a combat wedge to the front of Cyclops—kind of like wedge designs on BattleBots. If you can build a second version of Cyclops, you can try your hand at combat when all you can see is the view right in front of the bot. That's a lot more challenging than battle competitions where you can see the entire combat zone from a distance. Worried about damaging the camera when the robot flips over? Only compete on carpet or grass. You might also consider attaching a piece of bubble-wrap to the top of the digital camera to protect it from hitting the ground.

✔ *Navigate to hidden objects.* Try placing something somewhere in the room and challenge the robot driver to find it by driving around on a search and recover mission.

✔ *Go completely wireless.* Wouldn't it be great to abandon the wire plugging in the wireless transmitter? Yep, that's what I thought. But I couldn't find a battery-operated transmitter. If you find one, tell me about it and I'll put the information on my web site (in the section on this book) so everyone can try it out.

PROJECT 7

The Robot Arm

What You'll Need

✔ Lego MindStorms Robotic Invention System 2.0. As always, you can build the robot with an older set, but some of the steps will be slightly different, so you'll have to improvise.

✔ Foam board, about 32×40 inches

✔ Spare Lego blocks

✔ A pencil, pen, or marker

Time Required

About 10 hours

Difficulty

Above average. Because the robot arm has so many moving parts, it is pretty complicated, and its program is involved as well. You should have little trouble doing this project all on your own, though.

Project

Build a robotic arm using your Lego MindStorms. The arm will swivel around a base, able to pick up small objects and place them in a pile. This robot is more advanced than the robot arm at the end of the MindStorms "advanced Missions," since it remembers where it is stacking its objects, and can easily sort objects by color, making two or more piles.

Introduction

In this book, we've made some very cool robots that challenge the imagination. Robots that fight. Robots that explore. Solar-powered robots that deploy from a rocket. Robots equipped with video cameras. But when you get right down to it, most robots today have very simple jobs that don't involve fighting, flying, or navigating through mazes.

Instead, today's robots are typically bolted down to a factory floor and do the exact same job over and over again. Robots like these reduce human boredom and drudgery on assembly lines. They also do complicated tasks and dangerous jobs that are difficult for people to do. Right now, few robots are designed to do a large number of different tasks, like cook breakfast, vacuum the floor, *and* wash the car. Instead, a typical factory has *several* robots, each of which is designed to do just one thing, like shape a large piece of metal, weld a joint together, or sort objects rolling down an assembly line. When you combine all of those robots together, you can make something like a car with relatively little human labor.

In this project, we'll try to mimic that sort of robot. We'll make a robotic arm that's designed to sort colored objects into two piles: one pile for black and another pile for lighter-colored items.

The Robot

Figure 7-1 shows a picture of our robotic arm, which I've named Sorter. Sorter is similar to the robotic arm in the MindStorms Pro Challenges, but it does more. The robot arm starts in a central position and waits for you to place an object under the light sensor. After it sees an object, it decides whether it's black or a lighter color like blue or red. Then the arm drops, picks up the object, and turns to the left or right (depending on the color of the object it is holding). It drops the object and then rotates back to the starting position. This robot does a few interesting things that real robots in factories do:

✔ It can tell the difference between simple objects, such as by color

✔ It can remember where it is, so if it turns it can find its way back to its starting place

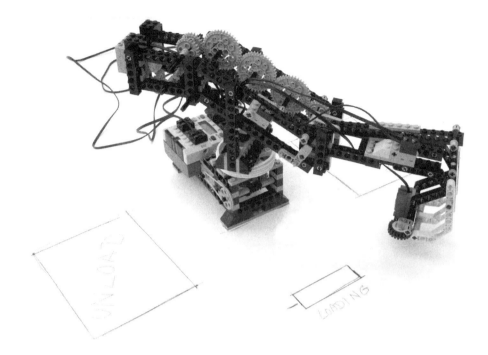

Figure 7-I
After you feed
Sorter a Lego, it
puts the block into
one of two piles
based on color.

The Plan

The first step is to build Sorter. You can build a robotic arm for Sorter exactly the same as the arm in the MindStorms Pro Challenge (so if you've already got it built, just leave it that way), but the arm in this chapter is a bit simpler, and has a few changes that make it perform better.

After Sorter is complete, we'll position it on a white board and mark the loading and unloading areas—these will simulate a "factory floor" for our robot. We'll finish by programming the robot. The program is a bit more elaborate than most of the other MindStorms projects we've done so far, but that's okay—it's easy enough to do on your own. The great thing about this project is that there are a lot of ways to change and improve it, so be sure to try some of the suggestions at the end of this chapter.

Building Sorter

Sorter is essentially a long robotic arm that's attached to a stationary base. We'll build it in two parts, then combine them toward the end of the assembly process. We'll start with the base.

Build the Base

Ready to get started? Follow these instructions:

1. Collect the various beams and blocks, as shown in the following picture, and then assemble them into the bottom of the robot base. Be sure to put the pair of angled blocks at each end of the two flat blocks, and connect the three beams using four round connectors before placing them on the top of the structure.

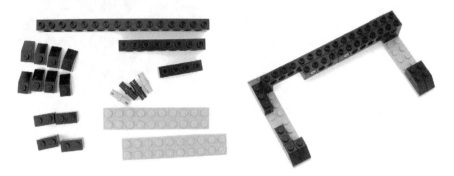

2. Add a motor to the end of the double beam and build the wall to support the motor, as shown.

3. Create the worm gear assembly using a 4X and a 3X rod. Slip the worm gear itself on the 4X rod and hold it in place with the gray cylinders. The worm gear is a key part of the robot's drivetrain, since it will connect to the motor via a pulley, and turn the gear that spins Sorter's arm. Hang on for a few steps, and you'll see it in action.

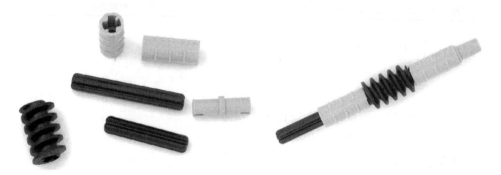

4. Now build the transmission gear. You'll need four 4X rods and an 8X rod. Insert the 4X rods into the ends of the two blue connectors.

When this gear turns, it'll turn the vertical axle (the 8X rod) that will eventually connect directly to the arm.

5. Insert both the worm gear and the transmission so they touch each other.

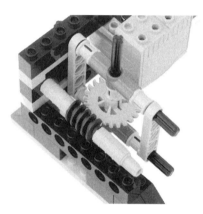

6. At this point, let's enclose the whole caboodle with the blocks, as shown, adding the 16X beam across the front and then building the wall on top. If you turn the worm gear's axle (it sticks out of the base), you should see the transmission axle turn at the same time.

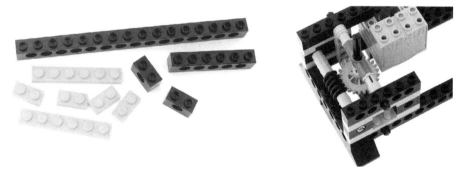

7. Add a power cord to the motor and then cap the top of the transmission housing with three thin 8X-long blocks, as shown. Then snap the RCX housing onto the base and plug the motor into port C. The base is done! Set it aside for a while.

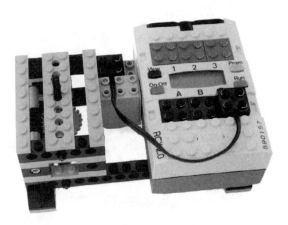

Build the Robot Arm

The base was a piece of cake to assemble, but the robot arm is a fairly intricate assembly. Pay close attention to the parts and their locations. We'll assemble a long train of gears that will make the arm move up and down when a motor mounted at the rear turns. And when the arm goes all the way down so the grabber reaches the table, it'll open automatically to grab an object. When the arm goes up, the grabber closes. Let's start with the grabber itself.

1. Using a 4X rod, attach the gray cylinders and narrow spacers to the end of a yellow arm. Add two 2X rods to the ends of the cylinders and then use a 3X rod to attach the two black beams to the end of the yellow arm.

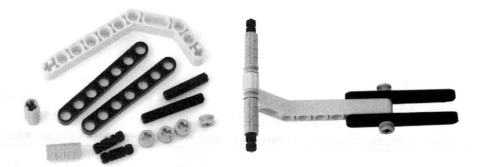

2. Add two black arms using a 10X rod at the yellow arm and an 8X rod at the end of the black arms. Cap one end of the 8X rod with the two connectors, as shown. As you'll see in the next step, the two spinning blocks will actually hold the light sensor in place.

3. Add the additional pair of black arms, inserting the gray connectors pointing inward, then add the yellow arms and cap the 10X rod at both ends. All three yellow arms should point the same way. Attach the light sensor and other connectors, as shown in the following picture.

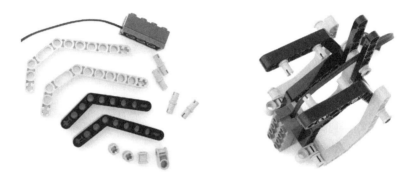

4. Now it's time to start building the long arm assembly. Snap the pair of 10X beams onto the connectors in the arms from the previous step. Then, add a third 10X beam to the outside of one arm, and add the blocks to the end of another arm, as shown. Use a pair of thin blocks immediately above and below the 10X beam.

5. Using a 6X beam, reinforce the outside of the blocks by mounting it vertically, as shown.

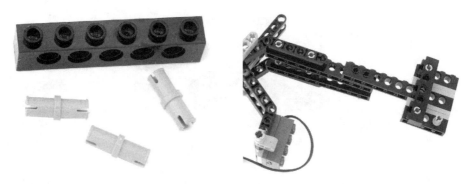

6. Use four thin blocks and a 4X beam to start to build up the other side of the arm. Also, position the remaining thin blocks—these will soon support a touch sensor.

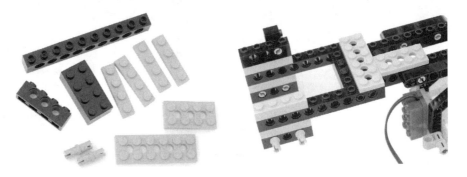

7. Now add a touch sensor to the small platform we've made at the end of the arm, pointing the sensor itself toward the grabber and reinforcing the structure with the angled blocks.

8. Attach a pair of 8X beams to the top of the grabber using a 5X rod. Use thin 6X blocks to hold the two beams together. At the other end of the beam, add the gear assembly using a 10X rod.

9. Add a 4X atop the two thin blocks on the other side of the arm, slipping the gear axle into both sides of the arm, as shown. Then, attach a 16X beam to the bottom of the arm using a connector and attach a 12X beam to the end of the 16X beam. Careful, it's getting long and tricky to manage!

10. Add the blocks and connectors, as shown, to the 12X beam at the end of the arm assembly. The rearmost blocks will hold the motor in place, while the other blocks will help support the top of the arm assembly. When you snap the thin blocks with the little flanges into place, be sure to put them closest to the 2X beam in the middle.

11. Attach a 12X beam to the top of the blocks and add the 6X "reinforcement" beam vertically on the outside of the assembly—but only add a connector to the top. Let it swing loose, because a gear axle will later go through the beam's hole at the bottom.

12. Now it's time to make another worm gear. This one will transfer power from the motor at the back of the arm to gears that run the length of the arm. Start by sliding the gear, connectors, spacers, and worm gear onto a 10X rod.

13. Next, slide two 8X rods and a 12X rod into position, then lock them in place with the beams, as shown.

14. Now add a pair of black arms to both sides of the worm gear assembly, connecting a gear to the worm gear with a 6X rod.

15. Slide the whole worm gear assembly onto the robot arm so that the long rod goes through the vertical beam on the outside of the wall.

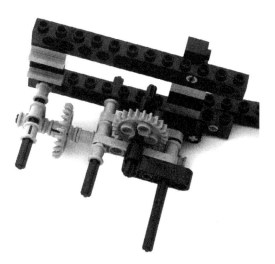

16. Let's build up the other side of the arm. Slide a 12X beam into place on the bottom of the arm assembly and add matching blocks to make it look like the other side you've already done—use pairs of thin blocks and remember to add the tin blocks with flanges to hold the motor in place. Then attach a gear to the motor and slide it into place at the back of the arm. Finally, attach a 16X beam to the top of the arm and add three 8X rods to the arm in the proper positions. Hold the middle rods in place with just one spacer on the inside of the beam, so the rods don't stick out of the other side.

17. Add the gears! Slide three gears onto the rods so they line up and make a gear train that runs from the front of the arm to the rear (but it won't connect to the worm gear yet).

18. Add two gears to the same 10X rod and position it above the worm gear assembly, as shown. Now you have a complete drivetrain that runs from the motor at the back all the way to the front of the arm.

19. Add a 12X beam to the top of the side wall at the rear of the arm. Place spacers on the two middle gear rods and position another 16X beam in place. Hold it in place with a single spacer at the front of the arm. It should look like this:

20. Now add 6X vertical beams to the three remaining positions at the rear of the arm, like this:

21. Add the touch sensor to the side of the robot arm. Slide a 4X rod through the sensor and beam, then use a short beam and connector on the other side to keep it from swiveling.

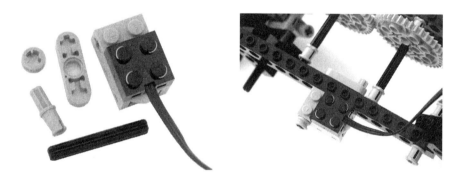

22. Next, add a 16X beam to the lower part of the arm. Mount the touch limiter at the end of it, as shown; the limiter will touch the touch sensor when the arm rotates, telling the robot that the arm can't go any higher.

23. Snap a pair of 12X beams onto the upper and lower beams of the arm, as shown. These act as the supports that hold the arm on top of the base.

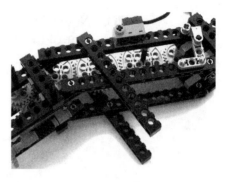

24. Turn the whole thing upside down and build a base onto the bottom of the arm supports, as shown.

25. Snap a 2X block onto the inside of the base with a connector, as shown; this will help hold a power extender in place.

26. Finish the arm support base by adding the remaining blocks, as shown in the following image.

27. Snap a pair of small wheels onto the supports near the light sensor, pointing down towards the floor. These guys help us hold blocks when it's time to pick stuff up.

28. Using the long connectors, attach the large wheel to the bottom of the arm extender base. That's it! The arm is complete, and now it's time to put it all together.

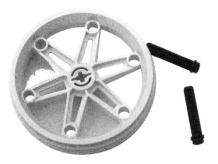

Connect the Arm and Base

Ready for the home stretch? We need to attach the two parts and wire it all together.

I. Take the arm in your hand and carefully slide the axle from the base into the bottom of the arm support base.

2. Connect the arm motor's power cable to the arm extender base, and then snap a short extension on top. Connect that cable to power port A on the RCX controller.

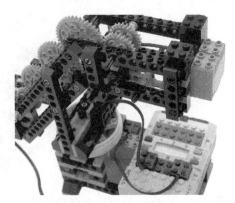

3. Connect the two touch sensors using a short power cord. Snap a long power cord onto the top and connect it to sensor port 1, with the wire facing away from the robot arm.

4. Connect the light sensor's power to a block on the underside of the arm, then attach a long power cord on top and run it to sensor port 3. To keep cables from getting tangled, be sure to run all the wires through the middle of the arm assembly.

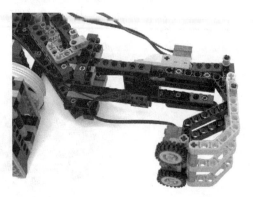

That's the whole thing; it should look like the robot pictured in Figure 7-2.

Figure 7-2
The completed
robot is ready for
programming.

Building the Factory Floor

Now it's time to create a small factory for our robot to live in. Get a large sheet of foam or poster board and position the robot in the middle. The board needs to be white—the brighter and cleaner it is, the better.

Using a pencil, pen, or very thick marker, trace the outline of the robot's base on the board. This way, we can easily position the robot correctly on the board anytime it gets moved.

Once you have marked the robot's position in the factory, it's time to mark some loading and unloading areas. For the loading area, do this:

1. Turn the worm gear axle on the side of the robot's base until the arm is pointed directly away from the RCS controller. After you turn the axle, add a pulley and put a narrow spacer on the motor. Then connect the motor to the pulley with a small rubber band. The robot should be positioned roughly like this:

2. Stick your finger in the rear of the robot arm and spin the motor until the arm settles down to the table.

3. Carefully check where the light sensor is located (it's in the middle of the blue block, pointed down at the table) and make a small mark at the edge of a wheel to indicate the centerline of the sensor. Then, make two more marks on the outside edges of the wheels.

4. Move the robot out of the way and draw a rectangle that's about as long as the distance between the two wheels and about a half-inch thick. This is our loading area—where we'll put our blocks for pick up.

5. Finally, put the robot back in place and draw two big squares on either side of the robot, like the ones in the next picture. These unloading areas are where the robot will drop off its load.

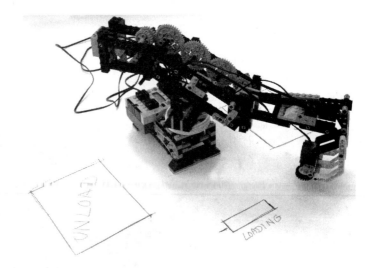

Programming Sorter

Ready to start programming the arm? Great—but first, let's figure out what we really want the arm to do. Here's the plan:

1. The robot waits for an object to appear under the light sensor.

2. When it senses something to haul, it lowers the arm and scoops it up.

3. Depending on the object's color, the arm rotates left or right and drops it off, making two separate piles.

4. The arm returns to the starting point and waits for a new object.

That's pretty much it—a piece of cake, right? But as we start to program the robot, we'll find out that it's a bit more complicated. We'll discover that we can't drop the arm straight down, for instance, because the grabber won't open until it touches the table. And that means it'll just end up pushing the object out of the way. So when we want to scoop something up, we need to swing out of the way to the left or to the right, lower down to the table so the grabber opens, then swing back to get the object.

Ready? Let's start.

I. Start The Robotics Invention System software on your PC and click on the programming option. When it asks you what kind of robot you want to program, click Pick a Robot and then, on the next screen, choose Robotic Arm.

2. Since we chose to build a robotic arm program, you'll find that a bunch of Big Blocks are already designed to move the arm from side-to-side and up and down. We don't have to program boring stuff like which way to turn the motor to activate the arm.

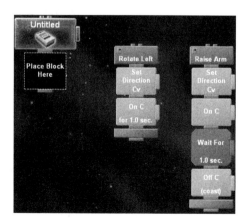

7

3. Our first step is to prepare the robot for scanning. The light sensor needs to be high enough off the factory floor to see the blocks. To set it at a reasonable height, let's start by raising it all the way to the top. Drag a Repeat Until block onto the program and place a Raise Arm block inside it. Set the Raise Arm to go up .1 seconds at a time, and configure it to Repeat Until it touches the touch sensor at port 1. We're kinda cheating; both touch sensors are located at port 1, but we'll never need to know if both are activated at the same time!

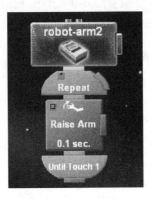

4. After the Repeat Until block, add a Stop Motors block to turn off the motor. Then add a Lower Arm block to the program and set it to run for 2.5 seconds. If you test this program now, you'll find that no matter where the arm starts, it'll go up to the touch sensor limit and then lower about halfway. It's now ready to look for a block.

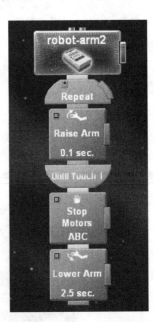

5. If we're really ready to start working, let's tell the human operator that the factory is open for business. Open Small Blocks, click Sound, and

drag a Tone block onto the program. When you hear the tone, Sorter
is ready to do some heavy (or light) lifting.

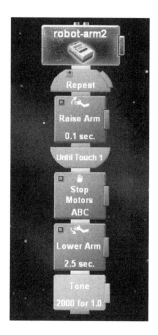

6. Now it's time to look for blocks. This is pretty easy. Just grab a Wait
Until block and set it for the light sensor on port 3. The sensor event
should be "dark," since we want to know when a block appears on
the white floor.

7. Later, we'll need to know exactly what color the block is so we can sort it. So, from the Set blocks, add a Set Variable block to the program and create a variable named "color." Set "color" to the value of the light sensor at port 3—it'll be a number from 1 to 100, where higher numbers are brighter and lower numbers are darker. Later, the variable called color will tell us the value of the block. While we're working on the block color, click Small Blocks and click Comm. Add a Display Value block to the program and set it to color. What will this do, you wonder? When the sensor sees a block, it'll show its value on the RCX box's LCD display. You'll be able to simply look at the robot to know what color the block is. Finally, drag a Beep block to the program so we'll hear a sound when the robot sees a block.

Now test what you've done so far. Download this program to the robot and test it by waving different color blocks under the light sensor. You'll have to restart the program on the robot every time you get a new block, since the program only looks for a color once each time. Have you encountered a problem? You have probably noticed that every block, whether it's black, green, red, or blue, is exactly the same value on the RCX controller. What's wrong?

If you think about it long enough, you might figure it out on your own, but I'll help. The light sensor is used to looking at the bright white factory floor, and when you put the block under its nose, it takes a moment for the sensor to adjust—like when you go outside after being in a dark movie theater and your eyes take a few seconds to get used to the light. To get this robot to accurately judge the color of a block, we need to wait a second or two before we take a reading. Insert a Wait For block under the Wait Until Light 3 block. Wait for 2 seconds before you set the color to the value of the light sensor. Test the program again and I think you'll get much better results.

All set? Let's continue:

I. Assuming you've inserted the Wait For block to slow down the color test, it's time for the robot to spring into action. We need to swing the robot out of the way before it's lowered to grab the object, so add a Rotate Right block and let it turn for 2 seconds.

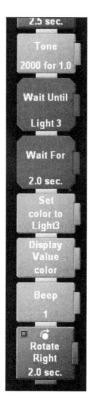

2. Add a Repeat Until block and insert a Lower Arm command inside it. We want to lower the arm a little bit at a time until it runs into the touch sensor on the front of the arm—that sensor tells us we've hit a limit on how far the arm can move.

3. Stop the motors with a Stop Motors block, then spin the arm back to where it started by rotating left. If all goes well, the arm should now be in position to grab the object it saw you place on the factory floor.

4. Now let's raise the arm up off the floor. Add a Repeat Until block and use it to raise the arm .1 seconds at a time until it touches the touch sensor again, as in the next image. When it feels the touch sensor go off, stop the motors.

5. Now that we're holding the object way up high in the air over the factory floor, we need to decide which pile to put the object in—the pile on the right or the pile on the left. The object's color will tell us which way to go, so we need a block that helps us make a decision. Drag the Yes or No block to the program and configure it for the variable color. But what value do we set it for? We don't know yet! Click OK to close the block up, because we need to take a short detour.

Test Block Colors

For Sorter to reliably tell the difference between black, blue, and red blocks, you need to test the blocks in lighting that's similar to the light you'll have when Sorter is working. So don't do this test at night and then try to run Sorter at noon; you'll have to quickly retest the blocks, make minor changes to the robot's program, and then run the program. Once you learn how to test the blocks for their color values, you could even make two copies of this program—one for day and one for evening, with the color values already set.

Drag a light sensor block onto the program, like a Wait Until block, and configure it to look for the light sensor on port 3. When you get to step 4 of the block setup, switch the darkness level from Automatic to Manual. Then turn on the robot and click Try It. After a few seconds, you should be able to see a little arrow on the screen that indicates the brightness of the factory floor—probably around 70. Place a black block under the light sensor and watch the value change. It should go way down, perhaps to 55 or 60. Then try some blue, green, or red blocks. See how they all have different color values?

After you've experimented for a bit, place a black block under the light sensor, wait a few seconds, and write down the value. Repeat this process for all the other blocks you have. When you're done, close the block and throw it away; you don't need it anymore.

Turn the Right Way

Now that we know the color values of the various blocks, we can finish the program.

1. Set the Yes or No block so that it checks to see if the variable color is more than the black block. In average daylight conditions, I found that my black blocks were about 55, while blue and red were both higher than 62. So I set it to put black in one pile and everything else in another pile.

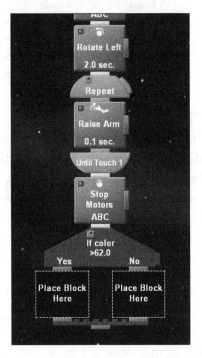

2. For nonblack blocks, we're going to turn to the right. We simply rotate right for 5 seconds, then stop the motor. We'll lower the arm a little at a time until we trip the touch sensor, and then stop the motors again. On the other side of Yes or No, we do exactly the same things for the black blocks, only we turn to the left instead.

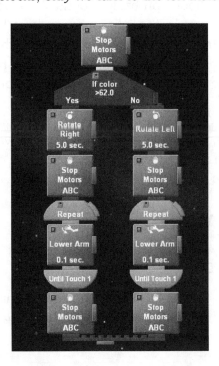

3. We're positioned over the unloading zone. We'll beep to let the operator know that the cargo has been dropped off, then rotate the opposite way, back to the loading zone. Stop the motors, and that's about all there is to it.

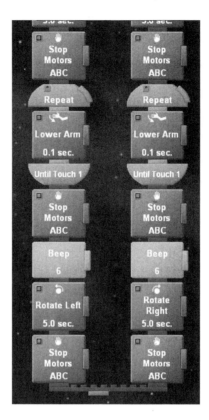

4. The program is complete, but it'll only carry a single block. Put the finishing touches on old Sorter by wrapping the entire program in a Repeat Forever block.

Improving Sorter

Sorter does a pretty good job. In fact, I've had fun just feeding it blocks over and over, watching the bot stack them into little piles. But there are all sorts of things you can do to improve this factory. Try some of these:

✔ *Build a delivery bot.* If you have a second MindStorms set or extra parts, try building a rover-style bot that automatically delivers blocks to the loading area for Sorter to sort. With a little programming, you can even "upgrade" Sweeper from the first project to deliver parts to Sorter.

✔ *Sort three colors into three different piles instead of two.*

✔ *Adjust the timing.* Do you notice a "drift?" Your motor may take you too far in one direction over and over, so your robot slowly starts making piles in the wrong positions. Adjust the timing so that the robot stays on track. Or, you might want to try using the light sensor to keep track of its position above the floor—think about ways to tell the arm where it is with marks on the foam board.

✔ *Make it interactive.* This is the coolest modification you can make to Sorter, and one I had lots of fun with. Try to design a version of Sorter that prompts you to place blocks under the light sensor in the proper order, senses the color brightness of each block, and automatically calibrates the program to tell the difference between blocks in the current lighting conditions. It could, perhaps, run the "calibration sequence" at the start of every sorting session.

Glossary

Actuator   An actuator is any kind of device that puts something into motion. A robot arm must have actuators that bend the elbow and move the wrist, for instance.

Animatronic   This is the word used to describe motorized puppets. You can see them in museums and at theme parks, where these elaborately-designed figures often act out history or depict a scene from a movie or book. Animatronics can be people, animals, space aliens, or even dinosaurs.

Artificial intelligence   Artificial intelligence is a quality that lets a computer or a robot behave as if it were human. True artificial intelligence (AI, for short) means programming a robot so that it really would have human-like intelligence, and possibly even human-like emotion. For the present, however, AI usually refers to programming a robot to simply act like it's human.

Assembly language   This is a programming language that is often considered to be the closest to actually "talking" to a computer in its own language. There are many programming languages in use, and most of them try to make the act of programming more like the human language. Assembly doesn't do that, so

Glossary

programmers have to think more like a computer to successfully write a program in that language.

Autonomous   An autonomous robot is one that isn't directly controlled by people or outside forces. Instead, it relies on its own programming to decide where to go, what to do, and how to react to the world around it. A successful autonomous robot needs careful programming and sensors that can tell it a lot about its environment.

Bug   A bug is a problem or an error in a robot or a computer program that makes it do the wrong thing, generate incorrect data, or otherwise stop working properly. The term dates back to the early days of computers when a computer glitch was traced back to a real, live bug that was found in a computer.

Chassis   A chassis is the frame of a motorized vehicle. It usually holds the motor in place, supports the wheels and body, and is the structure that gives the vehicle its strength.

CPU   The central processing unit, or just the "processor," for short, is the primary computer chip that acts as the brain of a computer or robot. The processor runs the computer program that gives a machine or robot its apparent intelligence.

Debug   When you fix the glitches in a computer program or robot design, you're debugging it.

Drivetrain   The drivetrain includes all the parts—usually a bunch of gears—that connect the motor to the wheels and allow the power of the motor to actually move the vehicle.

Gearbox   The gearbox is a casing that encloses a collection of gears. The gears in a gearbox usually change the power of the motor or change the direction that the power is transferred. A gearbox, for instance, can be used to turn an axle that's actually perpendicular to the motor's shaft.

Hexadecimal   Although people use a number system based on 10 (probably because we have ten fingers), computers rely on the hexadecimal number system. This system uses 16 digits, starting with zero. After 9, the next digits are A, B, C, F, E, and F. The letter F is the equivalent of the number 15.

LCD   A Liquid Crystal Display (or LCD) is a common kind of computer display that can show graphics or text. The display on the MindStorms RCX controller is a simple LCD display, and the large color screen built into a laptop computer is also an LCD.

Pathfinder In 1997, NASA sent a robot probe called Pathfinder to Mars. Pathfinder dropped a small, solar-powered rover onto the Martian surface. This robot, called Sojourner, drove around a small area of Mars doing scientific experiments. It was amazingly successful and inspired NASA to plan lots of other robot missions to Mars that may include larger rovers and robotic airplanes.

Payload A payload is something carried by something else. Rockets, for instance, carry a payload into space. The payload is usually a satellite or some sort of scientific probe.

Processor See CPU.

Program A program is a series of computer instructions that tell a computer or robot how to behave. Programs can be very simple or extremely elaborate, but all programs are written by human beings, and robots can't do anything unless the program tells them how.

Robot A robot is a reprogrammable, multifunctional device that can perform a variety of tasks. Read the first chapter of this book for more information about just what a robot can—and can't—be.

Roboticist A roboticist is a scientist or engineer who has made a career of designing robots.

Sensor A sensor is a device that can learn about its environment by monitoring a specific element of the world, like light, sound, touch, speed, temperature, or voltage. Your eyes are very advanced biological sensors that let you see.

Solar array A solar array is a collection of many solar cells. Solar cells, in turn, are metallic wafers that react to sunlight by generating electricity. You don't get a lot of power from a solar array, but it's "free" energy since you don't need batteries or fuel.

Subroutine A subroutine is a part of a computer program that contains related commands. Subroutines are often used to make a program easier to understand or to simplify doing the same steps over and over again. To make a program easier to read, for instance, a robot that needs to look down constantly to make sure it isn't about to fall down a flight of stairs would reference a "check for stairs" subroutine that really contains a few hundred lines of instructions.

Variable In mathematics and computer programming, a variable is a placeholder for a value that can change over time or that may not be known right at the start. If a robot needs to stop loading a truck when it places a certain

Glossary

number of objects inside, for instance, it needs to remember how many it has already loaded. It can track that number when it is stored in a variable.

Virtual   This is the term used to describe a simulated environment in a computer program. If you play a game in which you skateboard in a park, the park is a virtual place.

Worm gear   A worm gear is a special kind of gear that looks like a long, curvy groove in a rod or axle, as opposed to a regular gear, which looks like a wheel with teeth. Worm gears are usually used to turn regular gears, though.

Index

Index

Index

Index

Sorter. *See* robot arm
sound
    adding to combat robot, 91
    adding to robot arm, 174–175
    keeping score with, 86
stability, testing rocket, 111–112
Start Battle button, 125, 135
Start Match button, 126, 135
Starting Circle
    drawing route, 26–27
    envisioning program for, 28–30
    race course for robot racer, 24–25
Stop Motors block, robot arm, 174, 176
subroutines
    building Marauder, 131–133
    defined, 185
    FollowLine, 32–35
    making robots move/shoot with, 130
Sunbeam household robots, 5
Sweeper, 15. *See also* robot racer

T

television (TV)
    direct connection to, 148–149
    wireless connection to, 148–149
tests
    combat robot, 76, 83, 88–89
    Mars Pathfinder recovery system, 110–111
    Mars Pathfinder stability, 111–112
    programs, 36–37
    Sorter differentiating block colors, 179
    when adding new commands, 32
Thor robot. *See* combat robot
thought
    neural networks and, 12
    robot capacity for, 4
throttles, 153
timing, robot arm, 182
Timmy robot, 8–9
Tone block, robot arm, 175
touch sensor
    combat robot, hammer, 69–71
    combat robot, improving, 91
    robot arm, building, 162, 167
    robot arm, connecting to base, 170
    robot arm, programming, 174
Touch Sensor block, combat robots, 85
transmission, robot arm, 158–159
transmitters, wireless video, 149–152

tripods
    attaching to R/C car, 146–147
    videobot, 143–145
turns
    improving robot racers, 38
    programming robot racers, 35–36
turrets, 127
TV (television)
    direct connection to, 148–149
    wireless connection to, 148–149

V

variables
    defined, 185–186
    keeping score with, 86
    virtual robots and, 121
VCR
    direct connection to, 148–149
    wireless connection to, 149–152
videobots. *See* RC (remote-controlled) videobot
virtual robots
    combat. *See* combat on computer screen
    defined, 186
    overview of, 3

W

Wait For block
    combat robot, 81–83
    robot arm, 176
Wait Until block, robot arm, 175, 176
weight, testing virtual robot, 124
wheels
    collision avoidance bots, 46–47, 52, 57
    combat robot, 66–67
    gear locks and, 67–68
    Mars Pathfinder, 100–108
    robot arms, 169
worm gear
    assembling robot arm, 158–160
    building factory floor for robot arm, 171–172
    building robot arm, 164–165
    defined, 186

Y

Yes block, light sensor, 179–180

Z

zoom, R/C videobot, 153

INTERNATIONAL CONTACT INFORMATION

AUSTRALIA
McGraw-Hill Book Company Australia Pty. Ltd.
TEL +61-2-9415-9899
FAX +61-2-9415-5687
http://www.mcgraw-hill.com.au
books-it_sydney@mcgraw-hill.com

CANADA
McGraw-Hill Ryerson Ltd.
TEL +905-430-5000
FAX +905-430-5020
http://www.mcgrawhill.ca

**GREECE, MIDDLE EAST,
NORTHERN AFRICA**
McGraw-Hill Hellas
TEL +30-1-656-0990-3-4
FAX +30-1-654-5525

MEXICO (Also serving Latin America)
McGraw-Hill Interamericana Editores S.A. de C.V.
TEL +525-117-1583
FAX +525-117-1589
http://www.mcgraw-hill.com.mx
fernando_castellanos@mcgraw-hill.com

SINGAPORE (Serving Asia)
McGraw-Hill Book Company
TEL +65-863-1580
FAX +65-862-3354
http://www.mcgraw-hill.com.sg
mghasia@mcgraw-hill.com

SOUTH AFRICA
McGraw-Hill South Africa
TEL +27-11-622-7512
FAX +27-11-622-9045
robyn_swanepoel@mcgraw-hill.com

**UNITED KINGDOM & EUROPE
(Excluding Southern Europe)**
McGraw-Hill Education Europe
TEL +44-1-628-502500
FAX +44-1-628-770224
http://www.mcgraw-hill.co.uk
computing_neurope@mcgraw-hill.com

ALL OTHER INQUIRIES Contact:
Osborne/McGraw-Hill
TEL +1-510-549-6600
FAX +1-510-883-7600
http://www.osborne.com
omg_international@mcgraw-hill.com